CONTENTS

- Introduction to Software Testing —————————————————————————————3

- Methods of Software Testing and its types —————————————————————8

- Black Box Testing Types and Ways of Testing ——————————————————11

- Defect, Defect Tracking and Defect Life Cycle ——————————————————56

- Software Development Life Cycle ————————————————————————70

- Software Testing Life Cycle ————————————————————————————93

- Interview Questions ————————————————————————————————127

- Conclusion ————————————————————————————————————167

INTRODUCTION TO SOFTWARE TESTING

1. What is Software Testing?

- **The Process of finding defects** in a software we call it Software **testing**.
- **Verifying the functionality of an application against requirement Specification** called **Software Testing**.
- **Execution of a program with an intent to find a defect in a software** we call it **Software Testing**.

Example:

Let's Consider a **Real time example of Software testing** for an **E-Commerce website**:

Scenario: Testing the checkout process on an e-commerce website to ensure smooth and error-free transactions.

Case: Objective: Verify that users can successfully place an order and complete the checkout process without encountering any issues.

1. **Preconditions**:
   - Users have items added to their shopping cart.
   - User is logged into their account or proceeding as a guest.
   - Shipping address and payment information are valid and correctly entered.
2. **Steps to Execute the Test**:
   - Navigate to the shopping cart page.
   - Click on the "Checkout" or "Proceed to Checkout" button.
   - Enter or confirm shipping address details.
   - Select a shipping method (e.g., standard, expedited).
   - Enter payment information (credit card details, PayPal account, etc.).
   - Review the order summary for accuracy.
   - Confirm the order by clicking on the "Place Order" or similar button.
3. **Expected Results**:
   - The order should be processed successfully.
   - The user should receive an order confirmation page or email.
   - The inventory of purchased items should be updated accordingly.
   - Payment should be processed without errors.
   - If applicable, shipping details and tracking information should be provided to the user.
4. **Validation**:
   - Verify that the order confirmation page/email contains accurate details (items ordered, shipping address, payment method, total amount).
   - Check the inventory system to ensure that the purchased items are correctly deducted from available stock.
   - Monitor the payment gateway for successful transaction records.

5. **Edge Cases to Consider**:
    - Attempting to place an order with insufficient stock for one or more items.
    - Testing different payment methods (e.g., credit card, PayPal, gift card).
    - Simulating network interruptions or server delays during the checkout process.
    - Testing with various combinations of special characters and lengths in shipping address and payment fields.
6. **Additional Tests**:
    - Testing the website's responsiveness during peak traffic times (e.g., sales events, holidays).
    - Testing the recovery mechanism if the user's session times out during checkout.
    - Verifying that the correct taxes and shipping costs are applied based on the user's location and selected shipping method.

Example Outcome: If during testing it's found that after placing an order, the inventory is not updated correctly, or the user does not receive an order confirmation email, these would be considered **bugs**. The tester would then document these issues with steps to reproduce and share them with the development team for resolution.

This example demonstrates how software testing is crucial in ensuring that an e-commerce platform functions smoothly for users during critical actions like making a purchase.

2.Why do we need Software Testing?

- Each and Every software is developed to support one or other business. If there is a defect in the software then the customer will undergo severe loss to avoid the loss to the customer, we do Software Testing.
- To Improve the quality of the software we should do software testing.
- To check whether the software is working according to the customer requirement or not.

3.Why do we need a Dedicated Testing Team?

The efficiency or quality of testing differs from the development team to the testing team.

- As time increases for delivery of software then cost of the software automatically increases.

- There is a possibility of missing some requirement by the developing team, it can be avoided by cross checking which will be performed by testing team

- Works get divided, so quality of the work improves and time taken to deliver a software decreases
- Developers will be able to test the application only from the perspective of how they created the application, they will not be in a position to think out of the box.
- Developers as they build the application they will have an intention of ignoring minor issues.

4.Who does software Testing?

It depends on the process and the associated stakeholders of the projects. In the IT industry, large companies have a team with responsibilities to evaluate the developed software in the context of the given requirements.

- Software Tester
- Software Developer
- Project Lead/Manager
- End User

5.What are the types of software Testing?

Types of software Testing:

- Manual Testing
- Automation Testing

Manual Testing: Understanding the requirement specified by the customer and writing test cases and having the application to be tested without using any kind of program or tools.

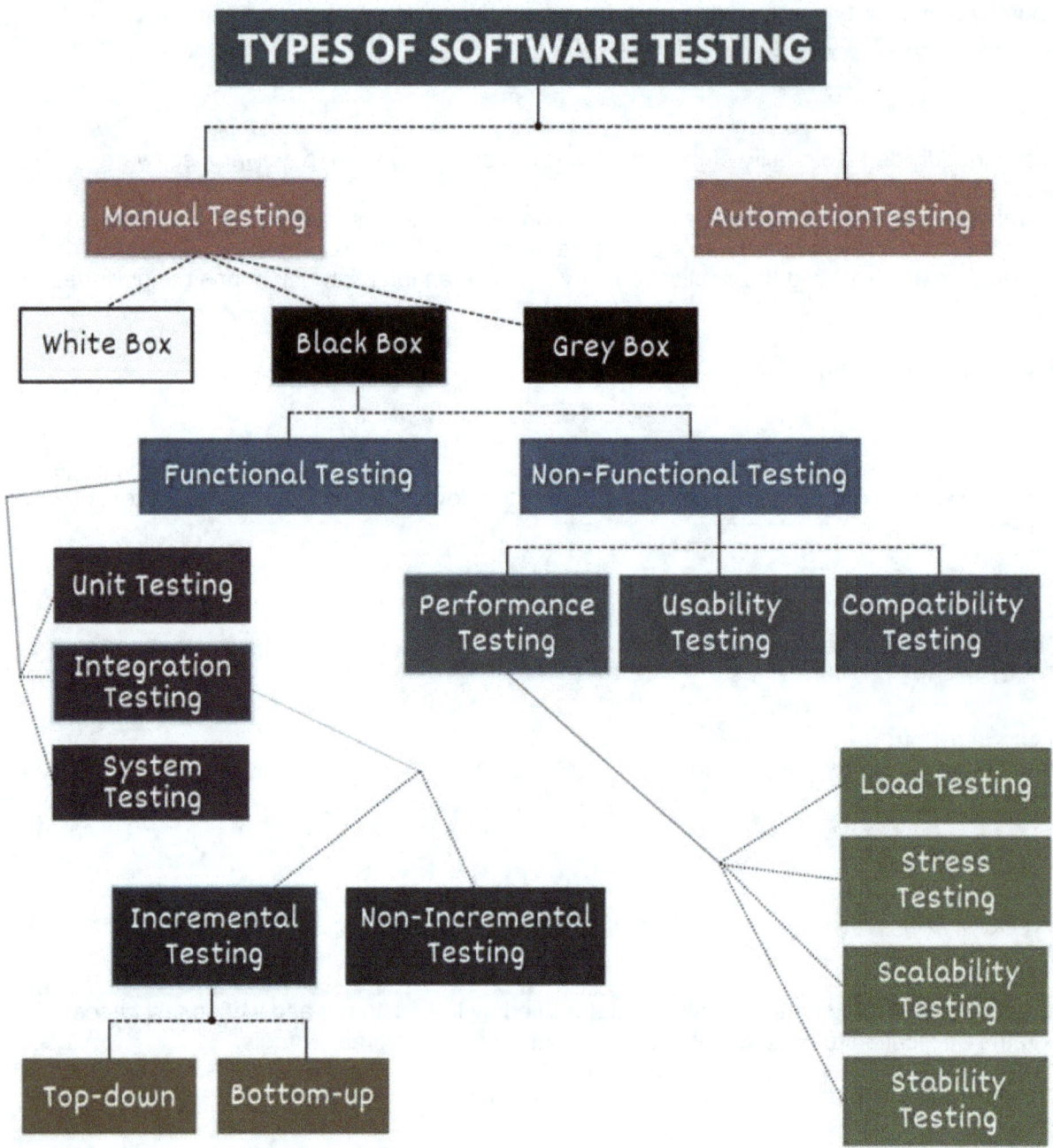

In this type, the tester takes over the role of an end user and tests the Software to identify any unexpected behavior or bug.

Testers use test plans, test cases or test scenarios to test the Software to ensure the completeness of testing.

Automation Testing: The test cases written by the manual tester engineer are being converted into a script or a program, and those scripts are used to test the application.

6.Difference between verification and validation?

Ensure that the software system meets all the functionality--->Verification

Ensure that functionalities meet the intended behavior----->Validation

Verification takes place first and includes the checking for documentation, code etc----->Verification

Validation occurs after verification and mainly involves the checking of the overall product---->Validation

Done by developers---->Verification.

Done by Testers----->Validation.

7.Is It 100% Testing is possible?

100 % testing is not possible – because the way testers test the product is different from the way customers use the product.

8.What are the concepts in software testing Companies?

Service based company: Companies that create software exclusively for one particular customer need are called service based companies. EX: TCS, CTS, Infosys, Accenture, Capgemini, HCL, Tech mahindra, Wipro, L&T etc.

In detail – Take an example of Indian Passport Seva. Currently the Indian Passport Seva project is being handled by TCS. (The customer will contact these companies and give his requirements).

Product based company: Companies that create software which can be used by N number of customers such as Microsoft, Oracle, Sun Solaris, Google, Mozilla etc.

Business Developer: They are responsible for contacting the customer and getting projects form the customer (Client).

Business Analyst: They are responsible for contacting the customers and getting requirements from the customer.

9.How do service and product based companies get to know about the requirements?

Thus service based companies have a dedicated exclusive customer (client) they can get the requirement from the customer but what about product based company?

They will get the requirement based on customer feedback.

- Market survey will be conducted by the experts of product based companies.
- By comparing with the competitors.
- By comparing earlier versions of software what they have launched.
- Due to technology development.

10. What are the types of software testing terminologies?

CRS: Customer Requirement Specification

BRS: Business Requirement Specification

BRD: Business Requirement Document

BS: Business Specification

SRS: Software Requirement Specification

FS: Functional Specification

Software Testing Methods and its types

There are 3 types of s/w testing, namely,

1) White box testing – also called unit testing or structural testing or glass box testing or transparent testing or open-box testing

2) Grey box testing

3) Black box testing – also called as functional testing or behavioral testing

White-box testing:

- White box testing analyzes **internal design, Code structure** and **working** of the **complete Software Product.**
- It is also called Unit testing, Open box Testing and Glass box Testing.
- It is the testing of each and every line of source code in the program.
- One Should have knowledge of programming to do white box Testing.
- It is almost done by Developers.

What are the types of white-box techniques?

- **Path Coverage /Testing:**

    1. Testing is dependent on the **program's control or flow structure**.
    2. All the possible points are defined with **entry and exit points** in the system.

- **Loop Testing:**

    Test the loops (for, while, do-while, etc.) for all the cycles and also check for terminating conditions if working properly and if the size of the condition is sufficient enough.

For example, let us consider a program where the developer has given about 1 lakh loops.

{

While (1,00,000)

……..

……..

}

We cannot test this manually for all 1 lakh cycles. So we write a small program,

Test A

{

……

…… }

Which checks for all 1 lakh loops. This Test A is known as unit test. The test program is written in the same language as the source code program.

- **Branch Coverage/Condition Testing:**

    Test all the logical conditions for both true and false values i.e, we check for both "if" and

"else" conditions.
If (condition) - true
{
…….
…….
}
Else - false
{
…..
…..
}
The program should work correctly for both conditions i.e, if condition is true, then else should be false and vice-versa.

- **Statement Coverage**:

- Statement coverage is the testing technique where you traverse all statements in code.
- It ensures that each statement of the code is executed at least once.
- Hence Each line of the verified.

Advantages of White box testing:

- White box Testing optimizes code so hidden errors can be identified.
- Test cases of white boxes can be easily automated.
- Easy detection of errors that Improve code quality.
- It covers most of the path and code of the software.

Disadvantages of White box Testing:

- White box Testing can be quite Complex, Expensive and time-consuming.
- Required professional resources with detailed understanding of programming.
- Missing functionalities cannot be detected.
- Redesign of code needs test cases to be written again.

Black Box Testing:

- Testing the Functionalities of **Software Applications without having Knowledge on Internal code structure**, Implementation details and Internal Paths.
- Testers give input value to examine its functionality and check whether the function is giving expected output or not.
- It is also known as Functional testing, behavior Testing and Closed box Testing.
- It is performed by Software Testers.
- Black box Testing Tools:Selenium,JMeter etc.

Types of black-box Testing:

- Functionality Testing
- Integration Testing
- System Testing
- Acceptance Testing
- Smoke Testing
- Ad Hoc Testing
- Regression Testing
- Performance Testing
- Compatibility Testing
- Exploratory Testing
- Globalization Testing
- Usability Testing

- **Advantages of Black Box Testing:**
- The Tester does not need to have more Functional Knowledge or Programming skills.
- It is Efficient for implementing the tests in the larger system.
- Tests are executed from the user's or client's point of view.
- It is used in finding the ambiguity and contradictions in the functional specification.

Disadvantages of Black box Testing:

- Without clear programming language test cases are difficult to implement.
- It does reveal the errors in the control structure.
- Working in the large sample space of inputs can be exhaustive and consumes a lot of time.

Grey Box Testing:

Grey box testing is a software testing technique that combines elements of both black box testing and white box testing. In grey box testing, the testers have partial knowledge of the internal workings of the system under test. They may have access to detailed design documents, architecture diagrams, or even the source code to some extent.

Key characteristics of grey box testing include:

1. **Limited Knowledge of Internal Structure:** Testers have access to some internal details of the system, but not as much as in white box testing. This allows them to design tests based on an understanding of how the system is structured and its expected behavior.

2. **Tests Based on System Design:** Test cases in grey box testing are often based on system design and architecture, focusing on critical paths, modules, or integration points where errors are more likely to occur.
3. **Benefits of Grey Box Testing:**
    - **Effective Test Design:** Testers can design more targeted and efficient test cases compared to pure black box testing.
    - **Better Coverage:** It allows for better coverage of critical areas of the application without needing to test every possible path or combination.
    - **Early Detection of Defects:** Since testers have some visibility into the internal structure, they can potentially detect defects early in the development cycle.
4. **Examples of Grey Box Testing:**
    - **Integration Testing:** Testing interactions between modules where knowledge of the interfaces and data flows is essential.
    - **API Testing:** Testing APIs where knowledge of the API specifications and data formats is required.
    - **Security Testing:** Testing security vulnerabilities that may require understanding of the application's architecture and potential attack vectors.

5. **Challenges of Grey Box Testing:**

    - **Dependency on Documentation:** Effective grey box testing relies on accurate and up-to-date documentation. Incomplete or inaccurate documentation can hinder test design and execution.
    - **Complexity:** It can be challenging to strike the right balance between the amount of knowledge required and maintaining the independence of testing activities.

Grey box testing is particularly useful in scenarios where having some insight into the internal workings of the system can significantly improve the quality and effectiveness of testing efforts, while still maintaining a degree of independence and objectivity in the testing process.

Difference between White Box Testing and Black Box Testing:

White Box Testing	Black Box Testing
Testing each and every line of source code we call it as White Box Testing.	Verifying the functionality of an application against requirement specification we call it as Black Box Testing.
White Box Testing is done by development engineers.	Black box Testing is Done by Test Engineers.
We need Good programming knowledge to do white Box Testing.	We don't need Good programming knowledge to do black Box Testing.
Under White Box Testing We can see the source code.	While doing black box testing we cannot see the source code.

Ways of Testing:

- Over Testing- Testing the application with the same **set of scenarios again and again** we called it as over testing.
- Under Testing- Testing the application with **insufficient set of Scenarios** we call it Under testing.
- Optimization Testing- Testing the application with a sufficient **set of scenarios** we call it Optimization testing.

Example of Over Testing:

Let us Consider the Account Text field and It should contain only 10 digits.

Testing only with numeric values of digits

Account Number:1234567890--> Valid data

Account Number:234567890--->Invalid data

Example of Under Testing:

Testing only with numeric values

Account Number:1234567890---->Valid data

Account Number:123234343----> Invalid data

Account Number:0 000------>Invalid data

Example of optimization Testing:

Testing with alphanumeric and symbols

Account Number:1234567890--->valid data

Account Number:@123172adb--->Invalid data

Account Number:1234--->Invalid data

Account Number:313243!--->Invalid data

Functionality Testing/Component Testing/Field level Testing:

Testing **Each and Every component thoroughly** (rigorously) against **requirement specifications** is known as functionality testing.

Thoroughly means By entering all the valid and invalid data.

In Testing we call data as Scenario's.

For Example:

consider a text field as Phone number and it should allow only 10 digits

Phone Number:98973356-invalid data

Phone Number:9283232222-invalid data

Phone Number:9876543562- valid data. This is the simplest example.

When we do Component Testing/When do we start Testing/Entry Criteria:

1. **After Unit Testing**: Unit testing focuses on testing individual units or components of the software in isolation. Once units have been tested independently (usually by developers), component testing verifies that these units work together correctly as larger components.

2. **Build should be installed properly:** This means that whatever software or application you are working with, its installation process should have been completed correctly without any errors or issues. The "build" refers to the compiled version of the software that is ready to be tested or deployed.

3. **Test cases should be ready:** Test cases are specific conditions and steps that are designed to verify the functionality and behavior of the software. Having them "ready" means that they have been prepared in advance, outlining what aspects of the software will be tested and how.

4. **Test data should be available:** Test data refers to the input data or scenarios that will be used during testing to validate different aspects of the software's performance and functionality. Having it "available" means that this data is accessible and prepared for use in the testing process.

5. **Resource should be available:** This generally refers to any necessary tools, environments, or personnel needed to carry out the testing or development tasks effectively. Resources could include hardware, software licenses, testing environments, and skilled personnel required for testing or troubleshooting.

The above points are the list of criteria that has to be satisfied to start an activity.

When do we Stop Testing/Exit Criteria:

1. We stop testing in two different cases
- If the **software quality good** Means:
- Software quality good means all the features requested by the customer should be ready.
- All the end to end business Scenario should work fine,
- There should be Zero blocker defect and Zero critical defect.
- If there are few bugs left out it should be within the limit set by the customer.
- You should have tested the software in an environment similar to the production environment.
- If the **Software Quality bad** means:
- If there are too many blocker and critical defects.
- If many end to end business scenarios are not working fine.
- If it is crossing the budget and also Schedule.
- **Exit Criteria:**
- Percentage of Test cases should be 90 %
- Percentage of Test cases pass should be 85%
- It should not cross more than 10 critical defects.
- It should not have more than 40 major defects.
- It should not cross 60 Minor defects.

Why do we Component Testing:

1. **Isolation of Components**: Component testing allows each component to be tested independently of the rest of the system. This isolation makes it easier to pinpoint and fix bugs or issues within specific components.

2. **Early Detection of Defects**: By testing components early in the development process, defects or issues can be identified and addressed sooner, reducing the cost and effort of fixing them later in the life cycle.

3. **Verification of Requirements**: Component testing verifies that each component meets its specified requirements and performs its intended functions correctly. This ensures that the software as a whole will meet the desired functionality.

4. **Improved Quality and Reliability**: Thoroughly tested components contribute to the overall quality and reliability of the software. When components work as expected in isolation, it increases confidence that they will function correctly when integrated.

5. **Security and Performance Validation**: Component testing can include tests to validate security measures (like input validation, authentication checks) and performance characteristics (such as response times, scalability under load). This helps ensure that the software is secure and performs well under various conditions.

6. **Facilitates Parallel Development**: When different teams or developers work on different components simultaneously, component testing allows them to verify their components independently. This supports parallel development efforts and integration later on.

In summary, component testing is crucial for ensuring the quality, functionality, security, and performance of individual software components before they are integrated into the larger system. It helps detect and resolve issues early, reduces risks associated with integration, and contributes to delivering a reliable and high-quality software product to users.

INTEGRATION TESTING:

Testing the data flow or interface between two features is known as Integration testing.

Take 2 features A & B. Send some data from A to B. Check if A is sending data and also check if B is receiving data.

Now let us consider the example of banking software

(Amount transfer).

Scenario 1 – Login as A to amount transfer – send 100 rs amount – message should be displayed saying 'amount transfer successful' – now logout as A and login as B – go to amount balance and check balance – balance is increased by 100 rs – thus integration test is successful.

Scenario 2 – also we check if amount balance has decreased by 100 rs in A

Scenario 3 – click on transactions – in A and B, messages should be displayed regarding the data and time of amount transfer.

How do we do Integration Testing?

- Understand the application thoroughly i.e., understand how each and every feature works. Also understand how each and every feature is related or linked to each other.
- Identify all possible scenarios
- Prioritize all the scenarios for execution
- Test all the scenarios
- If you find defects, communicate defect report to developers
- Do positive and negative integration testing.

Ways of Testing:

- Two way Integration Testing
- One way Integration Testing
- Zero way Integration Testing

Two way Integration Testing:

Checking the dataflow A to B module and B to A module we called it Two way integration testing.

One way Integration Testing:

There is data flow from A module to B module But There is no dataflow from B module to A module.

Zero way Integration Testing:

There is no dataflow from A to B module.

Types of Integration Testing:

- Incremental Integration Testing
- Non-Incremental Integration Testing

Under **Incremental Integration Testing we have two types**

- Top down Integration Testing.
- Bottom up Integration Testing.

Incremental Integration Testing:

Take two modules. Check if the data flow between the two is working fine or not. If it is working Then incrementally add the modules and Test the data flow between the modules.

Top down integration incremental Testing:

Incrementally add the modules and Test the data flow between the modules. Make sure that the module we are adding is a child of the previous one. Example: Child 3 is child of child 2 and so on.

Bottom Up integration incremental Testing:

Testing starts from the last child up to the parent. Incrementally add the modules and test the data flow between the modules. Make sure that module we are adding is the parent of the previous one.

Example:

The development team develops the s/w and sends it to the CEO of the testing team. The CEO then logs onto the s/w and creates the username and password and sends a mail to a manager and tells him to start testing the s/w. The manager then edits the username and password and creates a username and password and sends it to the engineer for testing. This hierarchy from CEO to Testing Engineer is top-down incremental integration testing.

Similarly, the testing engineer once he finishes testing sends a report to the manager, who then sends a report to the CEO. This is known as bottom-up incremental integration testing.

Non – incremental Integration Testing:

We use this method when,

a) When data flow is very complex.

b) When it is difficult to identify who is the parent and who is the child.

It is also called the Big – Bang method.

Combine all the modules at a shot and start testing the data flow between the modules. The disadvantage of this is that,

a) We may miss to test some of the interfaces

b) Root cause analysis of the defect is difficult – identifying the bug where it came from is a problem. We don't know the origin of the bug.

Example:

Let's consider the homepage of a Gmail inbox. When we click on an inbox link, we are transferred to the inbox page. Here we have to do non-incremental integration testing because there is no parent and child process here.

Stub is a dummy module which just receives data and generates a whole lot of expected data, but it behaves like a real module. When a data is sent from real module A to stub B, then B just accepts the data without validating and verifying the data and it generates expected results for the given data.

The function of a driver is it checks the data from A and sends it to stub and also checks the expected data from stub and sends it to A. Driver is one which sets up the test environment and takes care of communications, analyzes results and sends the report. We never use stubs and drivers in testing.

In WBT, bottom-up integration testing is preferred because writing drivers is easy. In black-box testing, no preference and depends on the application

System Testing:

It is end-to-end testing wherein the testing environment is similar to the production environment.

Here, we navigate through all the features of the test if the end business / end feature works. We just test the end feature and don't check for data flow or do functional testing and all.

Example:

Let us consider another example – insurance domain

When we buy a car, we have to obtain insurance on that. Let us consider that Bajaj Allianz Insurance company is the one which provides this car insurance. The insurance policy works in this way – for the 1st year when the car is bought, the insurance to be paid is Rs10000. For the 2nd year, the insurance must be renewed at Rs10000 again. For the 3rd year, if no claim has been made, then that customer is offered a discount of Rs1500 and he must have to renew the insurance at Rs8500 only. If an insurance claim has been made, then the insurance must be renewed at Rs10000 only. Bajaj Allianz Insurance wants the s/w to be developed which works as above. Thus it gives Wipro the CRS of above, to develop the software.

The development team develops the software

The above s/w works in this way. When the insurance agent logs in to the home page, he clicks on New Insurance and creates a new insurance policy for the new customer and fills up all the details and the new customer is assigned a IID (Insurance ID) 100. He then pays the insurance amount Rs10,000. After 1 year, when the time has come for renewal, then the agent logs in and clicks on Renew Insurance and enters the IID and renews insurance for Rs 10,000. The different test scenarios for the above are,

Scenario 1:

1) Login as Agent – click on New Insurance – Create IID 100 and Amount Rs10000

2) Change server date by 1 year

3) Login as agent – Click on Renew Insurance – and pay amount Rs 10,000

4) Change server date to 1 year

5) Login as Agent – Renew Insurance – IID 100 – Insurance Amount must be Rs 8500 since no claim has been made – thus the test is pass

Scenario 2:

Same as 1), 2), 3)

4) Before you renew for the 3rd year, Claim Insurance – Change server date to 1year.

5) Login as Agent – Renew IID 100 – Rs 10000 – No discount should be made because of the claim made above.

Scenario 3:

Same as 1), 2), 3) and 4) of 1st scenario

5) Before you renew 3rd time, - Click on Claim IID 100 , Rs 15,000 – Try to claim the amount – We shouldn't be able to claim this because the insurance has expired.

Thus, the actual definition of End-to-End testing can be given as – Take all possible end-to-end business flows and check whether in the software, all the scenarios are working or not. If it is working, then the product is ready to be launched.

Testing Environment and Why it should be similar to Production Environment ?

After the requirements have been collected and the design of the s/w has been developed, the CRS is then given to the development team for coding and building of the modules and the s/w. the development team stores all the modules and the code it builds in a development server which they name it REX (any name can be given to the server).

The development team builds module A of the s/w – does WBT – installs the s/w at http://qa.citibank.com - zips the code of module A and stores it in REX – the team lead of the development team then emails the zip file of module A to the test lead and tells him that the module A has been built and WBT has been performed and that they can start testing the module A – the test lead first unzips the module A and installs it in the testing team server named QA - the test lead then calls in the test engineers in his team and assigns them different parts of the module A for testing – this is the first cycle – the testing team do functional testing on A – let's say the testing team finds 100bugs in module A – for each bug found, the testing team prepares a report on the bug in a Word document file and each bug is assigned a number – like this, the testing team finds 100 bugs in the s/w – each test engineer when he finds a bug, he immediately emails bug report to the development team for defect repair – the testing team take 5 days to test module A.

The developers are reading the defect reports, goes through the code, fixes the problem – when testing team is testing s/w, the developers are fixing defects and also preparing another module and also doing WBT for the repaired program – now the developers fix majority of the defects(say 70) and also build module B – now the team lead of the development team installs the s/w at the above website, zips the code of the module B and sends a mail to the test lead containing the code – the test lead first uninstalls the old s/w and installs the new one containing module B and also repaired module A – and sends a mail to the test engineers in his team containing the new module and repaired module –

Whenever a new build comes in, the testing team concentrates on testing the new feature first – because the probability of finding the bugs is more, we expect more number of bugs in the new feature – as soon as new build comes in,

1. test new features

2. Do integration testing

3. retest all the fixed defects

4. test unchanged(old) feature to make sure that it is not broken

5. in the new build, we retest only fixed defects

6. Each test engineer retests only his bugs which are fixed, he is not responsible for other bugs found by other test engineers.

We find new bugs in old feature because –

1. fixing the bugs may lead to other bugs

2. adding new features (modules)

3. might have missed it in the earlier test cycle

In the second cycle – we do both functional and integration testing for A and B – we find 80 bugs – each bug is sent in a report of Word format – the developers repair about 40 bugs and also repair 5bugs of the remaining 30 bugs in the first test cycle.

Like this we carry on, and do about 20 cycles and reach a stage wherein the developers are developing the 20th build, say module L – now the testing team gets a server which is similar to the production server (real –time server on which the s/w will run at the client's place) – and install the s/w there – and they start off with system testing.

We start System Testing –

1. when the minimum number of features are ready

2. basic functionality of all the modules must be working

3. testing environment should be similar to production environment

We say that the product is ready for release when,

1. all the features requested by customer are ready

2. when all the functionality, integration and end-to-end scenarios are working fine

3. when there are no critical bugs

4. bugs are there, but all are minor and less number of bugs

5. By this time, we would have met the deadline or release date is very near.

The entire period right from collecting requirements to delivering the s/w to the client is known as release.

Each time a new module is built and an old module is tested is known as Build – testing.

Each build takes about 5 days or more or less.

The testing environment should be similar to production environment means,

1) The hardware should be similar to production –

a. The make (manufactured by) should be similar to production server (for ex, if the production server is HP, then test server should also be HP server)

b. Configuration and make must be similar, but different capacities i.e, number of CPUs).

2) The software should be similar to production –

a. The OS should be similar

b. Application server should be similar

c. Web server should be similar

d. Database server should be similar

3) Data should be similar to production –

1. We should create data similar to production

2. We should create a script to create a dummy data which is similar to a production environment.

ex – while 20000

create Username

create password into table customer

Run

In a real time environment, we may make lakhs of entries into the database. But, while testing we can't manually enter lakhs of entries, so we write a test script program which generates thousands of entries and thus can be used for testing.

In Testing environment, who is involved in installing the software?

o Test engineer (anybody from testing team)

o Anybody from development team

o Release engineer / Build engineer

Build – It is a piece of software which is copied, unzipped and installed at the testing server.

BIN

DEVELOPERS

All the programs will be compiled and then compressed (compressed file should be in zip, rar, war, gunzip, tar, jar) format and compressed file is called build which is copied and pasted in the test environment, installed and we start testing the software.

CASE 1: Test Engineer is installing the s/w

REX

Developers

Testing team

D : / Build / B01 / 01.zip

COMPRESS

BINARIES

COMPILE

01

01

01

01

D : / Builds / B01 / 01.zip

COMPRESS

COMPILE

Unzip it and installation is done by the Test Engineer

01.zip

Here, the developers once they get the requirements, they start developing the software. As each feature is built, the code is compiled, compressed and stored in a compressed format. In the above example, the first build is shown. As soon as the first build is ready, the development lead sends a mail to the test lead saying that the first build is ready and they can start testing it. He also gives the name of the server and the file in which the first build is stored. The test engineer then goes to the development server named Rex, and copies the file to the testing server. He then unzips the file, installs the s/w in the testing team server and allots the various features of the first build to be tested to the testing team.

CASE 2 : Develop is installing the software

When the developer is installing the s/w in the testing environment, the test engineer team should open the browser, copy the URL that is sent by the developer and paste it in the browser. If the developer installs, they'll give the username and password. The test lead then logs in using the given username and password, and creates his own username and password through which the testing team will login and start testing the software.

CASE 3 : Release engineer / Build Engineer

Release engineer is the one who manages the source code. If the developers are working at different locations, the release engineer first installs a VCT (Version Control Tool) like CVS, VSS, Clear Case and creates a folder in the tool. The developers should copy and paste the programs into that folder. Once the folder is locked, the developers can't send their programs when the folder is locked. Now, the release engineer will compile, compress and then build a s/w. Now he will only install the s/w inside the test environment (testing server) and send a mail to the testing team. The testing team then starts testing the s/w. If they find bugs, they report it to the developers. Once the developers fix these bugs and create a new module simultaneously, the folder will be unlocked and once again the developers send the programs into that folder which is locked after a new build has been developed.

Testing Team / Server

Release The folder will be locked and released later

Engineer

Creates

A folder

India Developers China Developers US developers

The release engineer performs 2 functions,

1. Manages source code

2. Creates a build and they install in the test environment

D : // Build / B01 / 01.zip

Compress

Compiled by

Release Engineer

The release engineer will copy and paste the build or the s/w and install the s/w inside the Test Environment.

Whenever the Release Engineer compiles the program, if the program does not compile then he will send the program back to the developers and ask them to check (or) not to send that program at that particular build.

When do we find Release Engineer (ing) ?

When the product is complex and big

When more number of developers are there

Once the product is ready to be released to the customer, then the release engineer will only release the product to the customer because he will be knowing which piece of software is working fine.

The Automatic release of the Build can also be done by the release engineer. He should write a script while compiling the program. If the release engineer finds any bugs in the program, he will go and see who has written that program and send that program to that developer (to fix the bug and send or not insert that program into that folder). All the activities done by a Release Engineer is called Release Management or Release Engineering. For the entire project to manage resources, we use VCT. Whenever the developers want to take the program out from the VCT, we use the check out option. Whenever the developer wants to insert a program into the VCT, we use the check in option.

Test cycle – Time spent on testing a build or software completely / time taken by the test engineer to completely test one software.

The developer writes a program and creates a module A and sends the module to the test engineer for testing. The test engineer tests the module and finds bugs and reports them to the developer. The developer fixes the bug and also creates a new module B. The developers only integrate module A & B and send it to the test engineer. The test engineer will uninstall the old s/w and install the new s/w and then do functional and integration testing for A & B. Whenever the new module is given for testing, if the test engineer catches bugs and reports it, the developers fix the bugs. But, the developer does not send that particular module for testing, instead he sends the fixed module along with the new module for testing.

Whenever the new build comes, we should always uninstall the old build and install the new build (latest build). Whenever we uninstall, all the accounts and data created will be deleted. So, whenever we install a new build – we must always login with manager Username and Password and create our own Username and Password.

When the first build comes in, immediately we find a bug and send it immediately to the development team. Thus, immediately we find a bug within a cycle. If another build comes within a cycle where the bug is fixed, then we call it respin.

We find respin – when the test engineer finds blocker defects / critical defects. For example, if the login feature itself is not working in gmail, then the test engineer cannot continue with his testing and it has to be fixed immediately – thus respin comes into picture. Inbox, Compose mail, Sent items are not blocker defects.

More number of respin in a cycle means the developer has not built the product properly.

5 days – 1st test cycle 5 days – 2nd test cycle 5 days – 3rd test cycle

Whenever the developer writes so many programs and sends the module for testing. The test engineer finds bugs and reports them to the developers. Once the developer comes to know the bug, he will look into the source code, if the problem is with only 1 program and that too only a few lines – he will fix the bug. He (the developer) will take the modified program, compile it and compress it into installable (format) and send a mail to the test engineer that a patch file has been sent. Once the test engineer starts installing this patch file, the program which had defect will be replaced by the corrected program.

Patch – is a piece of software which has only modified programs.

DEVELOPMENT SERVER TESTING SERVER

The above figure shows how a patch file is installed. Let us consider that the testing team has installed the build and started testing the s/w. They find bugs and report them to the development team. The block (shaded) is the defect program. The developer looks at the defect program and sees that it just needs a few minor changes. He makes the necessary changes, compiles it and compresses it and creates an installable (patch) and goes to the testing server and just installs the patch file which has the modified program. The testing team need not have to uninstall and install the build again.

Acceptance Testing:

Acceptance testing is done by end users. Here, they use the software for the business for a particular period of time and check whether the software can handle all kinds of real-time business scenarios / situations.

For Acceptance testing, let us consider the **example** shown below:

WIPRO FEDEX

Fed-ex with its requirements asks Wipro to develop the s/w and Wipro agrees to give the s/w in 2 releases like below,

25 crores   18 crores

Jan 2010 Sept 2010 to Sept 2010 Feb 2011

On September 8th, the test manager tells the project manager that there is a critical bug in the application which will take another 5 days to fix it.

But the project manager says you just deliver the application and by the time they implement it in Fed-ex, it takes another 25 days so we can fix the bugs or otherwise we will have to pay the penalty for each day after the said release day. Is this the real scenario ? – No. Then what happens, we will see now in 3 cases which really and who really does the acceptance testing.

CASE 1: here, we will discuss how the acceptance testing is done or how the test engineer testing becomes the acceptance testing here.

WBT

Usually, the actual flow of testing will be like above. But, here a small difference we see where the system testing or end-to-end testing becomes the acceptance testing. To understand this, follow the sequence below,

CODING

Functional Integration System

Testing Testing Testing

Product to Customer

Fed-ex gives the requirements and Wipro develops the s/w and do all testing and gives it to Fed-ex

Are the Fed-ex going to use the s/w as soon as they get from Wipro ? – NO, certainly not. Then what do they do ? – Observe,

Fed-ex, they have some group of Test Engineers and after they get the software, this team starts testing it. So, now we can understand that though the test engineer does the testing but it is done at customer level. This end-to-end testing is called ACCEPTANCE TESTING.

The difference between Wipro test engineers and Fed-ex test engineers are,

• The Wipro testing do Functional Testing, Integration Testing and System testing. But at Fed-ex, the testing team does only end-to-end testing / system testing.

The difference between end-to-end testing of Wipro and Fed-ex is,

• Fed-ex engineer is a domain expert

• Fed-ex engineer understands the business well

- Fed-ex engineer tests for real time data

- Fed-ex engineer is the one who gave the requirements.

To understand this, we see the example below. If the application format is like below,

NEW PARCEL

USERNAME:

PASSWORD:

FROM Address:

TO Address:

WEIGHT:

NEW PARCEL:

CHANGE ADDRESS:

DISPATCH

CANCEL

…

LOGOUT

SEND

CANCEL

PARCEL 1 Docket ID Produced

In the above example, after the product is given to Fed-Ex Test Engineers, they do testing and they know after the application has been filled above, it should produce a message saying "Parcel 1 Docket ID Produced". If this is not happening, they give back the application for fixing bugs. Now, the Fed-Ex checks whether this feature is there or not in the requirement. If it is there and Wipro has not done fix it, then Penalty Counts for Wipro from that day, whereas the TE at Wipro will not be knowing this and thus arises the difference in testing at Wipro and Fed-Ex.

Thus, the TE becomes END-USERS here and this testing is known as Acceptance Testing.

CASE 2: In this case, we see how the employees are becoming end-users and do acceptance testing.

The software is developed and tested at Wipro's place and then sent to Fed-ex. At Fed-Ex, they have less TEs and so it is not possible for them to do Acceptance testing. So, out of 400 employees of Fed-ex, Fed-ex gives the s/w to 40 employees and installs the product on their systems and asks them to start using the s/w and come up with bugs or issues.

Now, the 40 employees, they do dummy implementation (i.e, they implement the data into the application and also have the data written manually). Now, the employee here becomes the end-users and comes up with bugs and issues when using the s/w.

These issues are verified against requirements and now penalty is charged for Wipro (sometimes, penalty is charged on an hourly basis).

If the bug found is not as per requirement, then Fed-Ex can go for CR or RFE.

CR – Change Request – If the requirement has not been specified properly, then Fed-Ex gives the correct requirement and requests for change.

RFE – Request For Enhancement – if Fed-Ex feels that a particular module can be enhanced and developed in a better way, then they can send the CRS as RFE and Wipro goes on to make the necessary changes.

Thus, Acceptance Testing can also be defined as – end-to-end testing done by engineers sitting in customer's place. Here, they take real time scenarios and check whether the s/w works or not. Here also, we are able to take real time business scenarios because the end-users know how the business flow works.

We are getting more and more builds for Acceptance Testing means,

- The product quality which is delivered to customers is not good. Development and testing both are not good.

- After receiving the s/w, customer is getting more and more ideas, so he is asking for more and more changes

- The requirement which was given in the beginning is not clear.

CASE 3: Here, the Fed-ex customers become the end users.

Here, the s/w is developed and tested and implemented at Fed-ex production servers and thousands of users start using the s/w. This comprises the 1st release. When using the s/w, Fed-ex comes up with more features and enhancements and sends the CRS to Wipro who make the additional changes and modules and give it to Fed-ex.

Thus, what is happening here is – the requirements are collected by Fed-ex from customers and end-users and then the s/w is developed.

The number of cycles depends on,

- Number of features

- Complexity of features

- How new features affect old features

Hot fix – In a production environment, whenever the client finds critical bugs – developers fix the bugs – a small team of TEs test it – reinstall the s/w – client starts using the new s/w. This entire process is known as hot fix. It takes a few hours to 1 day.

For example, if the login feature itself is not working in the production environment, then the client immediately sends it for fixing which is done ASAP.

SLA – Service Level Agreement

Interim Release – (short release): Between 2 major releases – there is a short release of enhancements – this comes up when the client requires a small bunch of features very urgently. Out of 70 developers, around 10 come out and out of 30 TEs, around 3 come out – they develop and test the s/w – client does 1 short round of Acceptance testing – before adding it to the production environment – this interim could take just around 15 days to 1 month.

Why do we do Acceptance Testing?

- Under Business pressure the software company push the software tot the customer with lots and lots of critical bugs, Now if the customer releases the same software to the production environment then he might undergo severe loss to avoid the loss we do acceptance testing.
- We do acceptance testing to check whether the software contains critical defects.
- We do acceptance testing to check whether the software is matching the customer requirement or not.

When do we do Acceptance Testing?

Acceptance testing typically occurs towards the end of the software development lifecycle, after unit testing, integration testing, and system testing have been completed. It serves as a final validation step before the software is released to the end-users or customers. Here are the key points about when acceptance testing is conducted:

- **Completion of System Testing**: Acceptance testing is conducted after the system has undergone thorough testing at various levels, including unit testing (testing individual components), integration testing (testing the integration of components), and system testing (testing the entire system as a whole).

- **End of Development**: It typically happens when the development team considers the software to be feature-complete and stable enough for final validation.

- **Customer/User Involvement**: Acceptance testing involves participation from end-users or stakeholders who will be using the software in its production environment. Their feedback and approval are crucial before the software can be deployed.

- **Readiness for Deployment**: The purpose of acceptance testing is to ensure that the software meets the specified requirements and is ready for deployment into the production environment.

- **Multiple Rounds if Necessary**: Depending on the complexity of the software and the scope of changes or features, acceptance testing may involve multiple rounds to address any issues or changes identified during earlier rounds.

In summary, acceptance testing is done when the software is believed to be ready for use in the real-world environment, ensuring that it meets the expectations and needs of its users or customers before final deployment.

What:

- Alpha testing is conducted by the internal development team or a QA team within the organization.
- It focuses on testing the software application in a controlled environment where developers have access to the source code and can closely monitor the software's performance.

When:

- Alpha testing is typically conducted before beta testing, often towards the end of the development phase but before the software is released to external users or customers.
- It aims to identify bugs, usability issues, and other potential problems before moving to the next phase.

Who:

- Alpha testing is done by the internal team of developers, testers, and quality assurance personnel.
- They simulate real-world usage scenarios and test the software under various conditions to ensure it meets the defined requirements and functions correctly.

Beta Testing:

What:

- Beta testing involves releasing the software to a selected group of external users or customers who are not part of the development team.
- The software is tested in a real-world environment that closely resembles how it will be used by end-users.

When:

- Beta testing occurs after alpha testing and often after initial bug fixes and improvements identified during alpha testing have been implemented.
- It serves as a broader test of the software's usability, performance, and reliability in diverse environments.

Who:

- Beta testing is conducted by a group of external users or customers who volunteer or are selected to participate in the testing phase.
- These testers provide feedback, report bugs, and suggest improvements based on their experiences with the software.

*** SMOKE TESTING or SANITY TESTING or DRY RUN or SKIM TESTING or BUILD VERIFICATION TESTING

Testing the basic or critical features of an application before doing thorough testing or rigorous testing is called smoke testing.

It is also called Build Verification Testing – because we check whether the build is broken or not.

Whenever a new build comes in, we always start with smoke testing, because for every new build – there might be some changes which might have broken a major feature (fixing the bug or adding a new feature could have affected a major portion of the original software).

In smoke testing, we do only positive testing – we enter only valid data and not invalid data.

Why do we do Smoke Testing?

- We do smoke testing to check whether the build is Testable or not.
- We do smoke testing to find all the basic and critical defects of a software application.
- We do Smoke Testing to check whether the software is properly installed or not.
- It is a kind of health check of a software. We do this to check Whether we received any broken build.

When do we do smoke testing?

- As soon as the developers give the build to the testing team we start doing smoke testing.
- Before starting acceptance testing, They will do smoke testing to check whether they have received a complete build.
- We do smoke testing to check whether the product is installed properly in the production environment.
- In Certain projects developers will also smoke testing before giving build to testing team.

How do we manage Smoke Testing?

- We manage doing Smoke Testing by writing smoke test cases and smoke automation test scripts.

Example of Smoke Testing:

Scenario: A software development team has completed a major update to an e-commerce website that includes changes to the user interface, payment processing, and product search functionality. Before conducting detailed testing, they decide to perform smoke testing to ensure basic functionality is working correctly.

Process:

Objective: The objective of smoke testing here is to verify that the essential functionalities of the e-commerce website are operational and stable after the recent update.

1. **Test Cases**:

- **Homepage Access**: Verify that the homepage of the e-commerce website loads without any errors.
- **User Registration**: Check if a new user can successfully register an account.
- **Login Functionality**: Ensure existing users can log in to their accounts without issues.
- **Product Search**: Verify that the product search functionality returns relevant results.
- **Add to Cart**: Check if users can add items to their shopping cart.
- **Checkout Process**: Ensure that users can proceed through the checkout process, including entering shipping and payment information.
- **Payment Processing**: Verify that payments can be processed successfully using different payment methods (e.g., credit card, PayPal).
- **Order Confirmation**: Check if users receive order confirmation emails after completing a purchase.

2. **Execution**:
   - The QA team executes these predefined smoke tests immediately after the deployment of the updated e-commerce website.
   - Automated scripts or manual testing may be used depending on the complexity and criticality of each test case.

3. **Verification**:
   - If all smoke tests pass without encountering critical issues, it indicates that the basic functionalities of the e-commerce website are working as expected after the update.
   - If any smoke test fails, it indicates a potential significant issue that needs immediate attention before proceeding with further testing or releasing the update to users.

Outcome:

Upon successful completion of smoke testing, the development team gains confidence that the core functionalities of the e-commerce website are intact and operational. This allows them to proceed with more comprehensive testing, such as regression testing and user acceptance testing, to ensure the overall quality of the updated software.

Summary:

Smoke testing acts as a preliminary check to verify that the basic and critical functionalities of the software are working correctly after a new build or update. It helps identify show-stopping issues early in the testing process, ensuring that further testing efforts can be focused on areas beyond basic functionality.

Sanity Testing

In this section, we are going to understand the working of sanity testing, which is used to check whether the bugs have been fixed after the build or not.

And we also learn about **its process, why we need to perform the sanity testing, the objective of sanity testing, real-time examples, various attributes of sanity testing, advantages, and disadvantages.**

What is Sanity Testing?

Generally, Sanity testing is performed on stable builds and it is also known as a variant of [regression testing](#).

Sanity testing was performed when we are receiving software build (with minor code changes) from the development team. It is a checkpoint to assess if testing for the build can proceed or not.

PlayNextMuteCurrent TimeÂ 0:00/DurationÂ 18:10 Loaded: 2.94%Â Fullscreen

In other words, we can say that sanity testing is performed to make sure that all the defects have been solved and no added issues come into the presence because of these modifications.

Sanity testing also ensures that the modification in the code or functions does not affect the associated modules. Consequently, it can be applied only on connected modules that can be impacted.

The Objective of Sanity Testing

The key objective of implementing sanity testing is to fulfill the following aspects:

- The primary aim of executing the sanity testing is to define that the planned features work unevenly as expected. If the sanity test fails, the build is refused to save the costs and time complexity in more severe testing.
- The execution of sanity testing makes sure that new modifications don't change the software's current functionalities.
- It also validates the accuracy of the newly added features and components.

Attributes of Sanity Testing

For understanding the fundamentals of the **sanity testing techniques**, we have to learn their attributes and several other components. Hence, following are some of the important features of Sanity testing:

- **Narrow and deep**
- **A Subset of Regression Testing**
- **Unscripted**
- **Not documented**
- **Performed by testers**

Narrow and deep

In software testing, sanity testing is a **narrow and deep** method where limited components are protected deeply.

Subcategory of Regression Testing

It is a subdivision of **regression testing**, which mainly emphases on the less important unit of the application.

It is used to test the application efficiency under the requirements of the modification or new features that have been executed.

Unscripted

Generally, sanity testing is unscripted.

Not documented

Typically, sanity testing cannot be documented.

Performed by test engineers

Usually, Sanity testing is done by the test engineers.

Sanity Testing Process

The main purpose of performing sanity testing is to check the incorrect outcomes or defects which are not existing in component procedures. And also, ensure that the newly added features may not affect the functionalities of current features.

Therefore, we need to follow the below steps to implement the sanity testing process gradually:

- **Identification**
- **Evaluation**
- **Testing**

Step1: Identification

The first step in the sanity testing process is **Identification**, where we detect the newly added components and features as well as the modification presented in the code while fixing the bug.

Step2: Evaluation

After completing the identification step, we will analyze newly implemented components, attributes and modify them to check their intended and appropriate working as per the given requirements.

Step3: Testing

Once the identification and evaluation step are successfully processed, we will move to the next step, which is **testing**.

In this step, we inspect and assess all the linked parameters, components, and essentials of the above analyzed attributes and modify them to make sure that they are working fine.

If all the above steps are working fine, the build can be subjected to more detailed and exhausting testing, and the release can be passed for thorough testing.

Who executes the Sanity testing?

Generally, a sanity test case is executed by the **test engineers.**

When do we need to perform Sanity testing?

There are no such hard and fast software testing rules to execute the sanity tests process.

It is a quick process of testing the application as it does not include the scripting any of the test cases.

A Sanity testing is a narrow regression test that emphasizes specific areas of the component. And if we encounter the below two conditions, we needed to execute one round of sanity testing, and those conditions are as follows:

Case1

We go for sanity testing whenever there is an improvement in the functionality of the specified software.

Case2

Whenever the bugs have been fixed, or a new feature added, we need to perform sanity testing in order to check whether the application is still working fine or not.

Examples of Sanity Testing

For our better understanding of sanity testing, we will see the below example:

Example 1

Suppose we have an **e-commerce application**, which contains several modules, but here, we mainly concentrate on only a few modules such as **the login page, the home page, the new user creation page, the user profile page, etc.**

- While a new user tries to login into the application, he/she is not able to log in, as there is a bug in the **login page**.
- Because the **password field** in the **login module** accepts less than four alpha-numeric characters and based on the specification, the password field should not be accepted below 7-8 characters.
- Thus, it is considered as bug, which is reported by the testing team to the development team to fix it.

- Once the development team fixes the specified bug and reports back to the testing team, the testing team tests the same feature to verify that the modification that happens in the code is working fine or not.
- And the testing team also verifies that the particular modification does not impact other related functionalities.
- To modify the **password** on the user **profile page** there is a process.
- As part of the sanity testing process, we must authenticate the **login page** and the **profile page** to confirm that the changes are working fine at both the places.

Advantages and Disadvantages of Sanity Testing

Below are some of the vital benefits and drawbacks of Sanity testing.

Advantages of Sanity Testing

Some of the dynamic benefits of performing sanity testing are as follows:

Sanity testing is easy to understand and implement.

- It helps us to find any deployment or compilation issues.
- It is less expensive as compared to other types of software testing.
- It helps in rapidly finding the bugs in the core functionality.
- There is no documentation mandatory for sanity testing, that's why it can be executed in less time.
- The execution of sanity testing will help us save unnecessary testing effort and time because it only focuses on one or a few functionality areas.
- Sanity testing helps in detecting the missing dependent objects.

Disadvantages of Sanity testing

Following are the drawbacks of sanity testing:

- It's become a very complex process for the developers to understand how to fix the defects acknowledged throughout the sanity testing if they do not follow the design structure level.
- All the test cases are not covered under sanity testing.
- It is emphasized only on the statement and functions of the application.
- We do not have future references since the sanity testing is unscripted.
- It became a complex process to find any other components as sanity testing is executed only for some limited features.

Overview

In this tutorial, we learned the execution of the sanity testing, real-time examples, benefits, and drawbacks.

Sanity testing is implemented when a new functionality, modification request, or bug fix is executed in the program.

It is a **narrow and deep** testing process that is intensive only on those components where the modification has impacted.

Sanity testing is beneficial as it provides various advantages like, it offers a quick assessment of the quality of software release.

Sanity testing allows us to check the application's small functionality if a minor change occurs in the software.

AD – HOC Testing (Gorilla Testing):

Testing the **application randomly** is called Ad-hoc testing.

Why do we do Ad-hoc testing?

1) End-users use the application randomly and he may see a defect, but professional TE uses the application systematically so he may not find the same defect. In order to avoid this scenario, TE should go and then test the application randomly (i.e., behave like an end-user and test).

2) The Development team looks at the requirements and builds the product. The Testing Team also looks at the requirements and does the testing. By this method, the Testing Team may not catch many bugs. They think everything works fine. In order to avoid this, we do random testing behaving like end-users.

3) Ad-hoc is testing where we don't follow the requirements (we just randomly check the application). Since we don't follow requirements, we don't write test cases.

Examples of Ad-Hoc testing for Gmail:

1) Login to Gmail using a valid username and password. Logout from Gmail. Click on Back button. It should not go back to the Inbox page. If it does, then it is a JavaScript error and it is a bug. It should go back to the Login page and say the session expired.

2) Login to the Gmail homepage using a valid username and password. Once we are in the Inbox page, copy the URL of the inbox which is in the address bar of the homepage and paste it in Notepad file. Logout from Gmail. Now, open the browser page and paste the URL of the inbox in the address bar. It should not go to the inbox, instead it must go to the welcome page of Gmail.

3) Login into Gmail. Go to Settings and Change Passwords. Set the old password only as the new password and see what happens.

NOTE:

• Ad-hoc testing is basically **negative testing** because we are testing against requirements (out of requirements).

- Here, the objective is to somehow break the product.

When to do Ad-Hoc testing?

- Whenever we are free, we do Ad-hoc testing. i.e., developers develop the application and give it to testing team. Testing team is given 15 days to do FT. In that he spends 12 days doing FT and another 3 days he does Ad-hoc testing. We must always do Ad-hoc testing in the last because we always 1st concentrate on customer satisfaction

- After testing as per requirements, then we start with ad-hoc testing.

- When a good scenario comes, we can stop FT, IT, ST and try that scenario for Ad-hoc testing. But we should not spend more time doing Ad-hoc testing and immediately resume with formal testing.

- If there are more such scenarios, then we record it and do it at the last when we have time.

Compatibility Testing:

Testing the **functionality of an application in different Software and hardware environment** is called Compatibility Testing.

Why do we do compatibility Testing?

- We do compatibility testing to check whether features are working consistency in all the platforms.
- Developers would have written common code and they claim that it works in all the platforms or developer may write platform specific code and says it will works in respective platforms, In this case we have to test the software to make sure it works in different platforms.

When do we do Compatibility Testing?

- When the software is functionally stable in the base platform then we think about testing the software in different platforms.

How to do Compatibility Testing?

It depends on the kind of application, There are three kinds of application, They are

- Standalone application
- Client Server application
- Web application

1. Standalone application:

Applications that can be used by only one user at a time and also this kind of application internet and server is not required. This kind of application is called a standalone application. Example: Camera, Calculator, Note pad etc.,

2. Client Server application:

Here we have two kinds of software, One is client software and other is server software. We will interact with server software using client software. Here internet and service is required.

NOTE:

We will do compatibility testing on client software not on server software.

3. Web Application:

It is a kind of client server application. Here the browser acts like a client.

Any application which is accessed by opening the browser and entering the URL is called a Web application.

How will they allocate work while doing Compatibility Testing?

Each Test engineer will get a chance to compare their bunch of features in different platforms, so that he can identify more defects.

What Kind of defect can we expect while doing compatibility testing?

- Scattered content

- Alignment issues

- Broken frames

- Change in look and feel of the application

- Object overlapping

- Change in font size, style and color

- Object overlapping

Example of compatibility Testing:

Scenario: A software development company has developed a new mobile application designed for users to track their fitness activities. Before launching the app, they need to ensure it works seamlessly across various devices and operating systems that their target audience commonly uses.

Objective: The objective of compatibility testing in this scenario is to verify that the fitness tracking app functions correctly on different devices and operating system versions.

Test Cases:

1. **Device Compatibility**:

- Test the app on popular smartphones (e.g., iPhone 11, Samsung Galaxy S20, Google Pixel 5) to ensure it renders properly and all features work as expected.
- Verify compatibility across different screen sizes and resolutions.

2. **Operating System Compatibility**:
   - Test the app on different versions of operating systems such as iOS (e.g., iOS 14, iOS 15) and Android (e.g., Android 10, Android 11).
   - Verify that the app functions correctly and is optimized for each operating system's features and behaviors.

3. **Browser Compatibility (if applicable)**:
   - If the app has a web version or uses a web interface, test its compatibility across different web browsers (e.g., Chrome, Firefox, Safari, Edge).
   - Ensure the app displays properly and functions correctly in each browser without any layout or functionality issues.

4. **Performance across Network Conditions**:
   - Test the app's performance under varying network conditions, such as 3G, 4G, and Wi-Fi.
   - Verify that the app loads quickly and functions smoothly even with varying levels of network latency and bandwidth.

5. **Integration with Third-Party Devices and Services**:
   - If the fitness tracking app integrates with external devices (e.g., fitness trackers, heart rate monitors), test compatibility and functionality with these devices.
   - Ensure that data synchronization and communication between the app and external devices work seamlessly.

Execution:

- Testers simulate real-world usage scenarios on different devices and environments.
- They may use emulators, simulators, or actual physical devices to conduct compatibility tests.

Outcome:

- Compatibility testing ensures that the fitness tracking app works reliably across a wide range of devices and operating systems commonly used by its target users.
- Any compatibility issues identified during testing are reported, prioritized, and addressed by the development team to ensure a smooth user experience across all supported platforms.

Summary:

Compatibility testing is essential to validate that a software application functions correctly across diverse environments and configurations. In this example, ensuring the fitness tracking app's compatibility across various devices, operating systems, and network conditions helps deliver a robust and reliable product to users.

Usability Testing:

Testing the **user friendliness of an application** is called usability testing.

How to do usability testing?

- I will check look and feel of the application
- I will check whether it simple to understand or not
- Important Features /Frequently used features must be given to the user within three clicks.

When is Usability Testing Conducted?

Usability testing can occur at various stages of the software development lifecycle, including:

During Development:

- **Early Stages**: Usability testing can begin with prototypes or early versions of the software to gather feedback on initial designs and concepts.

2. **Before Release**:
   - **Mid to Late Development**: It is often conducted when the software is nearing completion but before it is released to users. This allows time for improvements based on feedback.
3. **Post-Release (Iterative)**:
   - **Ongoing**: Usability testing may continue after the initial release to refine and enhance the user experience based on real-world usage and feedback.

Who Performs Usability Testing?

Usability testing is typically performed by:

- **Usability Experts**: Experienced professionals who specialize in usability testing methodologies and user experience design. They design the test scenarios, conduct the tests, and analyze the results

- **User Experience (UX) Designers**: Professionals who focus on designing intuitive and user-friendly interfaces. They often lead or participate in usability testing to validate design decisions.

- **Testers and Quality Assurance (QA) Teams**: They may conduct usability testing as part of broader testing efforts, ensuring that usability issues are identified alongside functional and performance testing.

- **End Users**: In some cases, actual users of the software application or website are involved in usability testing. Their feedback provides valuable insights into how real users interact with the product.

Example Scenario:

Scenario: A team is developing a new mobile banking application aimed at making it easier for customers to manage their finances on the go.

- **What**: Usability testing would involve tasks such as logging in, transferring funds between accounts, paying bills, and viewing transaction history.

- **When**: The team conducts usability testing during the development phase to identify any usability issues and iteratively improve the app's interface and functionality.

- **Who**: Usability experts lead the testing, observing how testers (potentially including end-users) navigate the app and gathering feedback on ease of use, clarity of instructions, and overall user satisfaction.

Summary:

Usability testing is crucial for ensuring that software applications and websites meet user expectations for ease of use and functionality. It involves evaluating the user interface and experience through various testing techniques, aiming to enhance usability and overall user satisfaction.

EXPLORATORY TESTING:

"Explore the application, understand the features, based on understanding, identify all possible scenarios, document the scenarios, based on the identified scenarios and Test the application

Example:

Add user

Edit User

List User

Sales

Here Add User, Edit User, List User are developed and tested as per requirements, but few features like Sales feature are not available in CRS. So Our Testers will understand the sales feature thoroughly and whenever a new build comes – He starts to test the sales features based on exploratory.

Ex: Exploring Gmail, Invoice and Tested.

Chances are there, we might misunderstand a feature as defect / Defect as a feature. If a feature is missing. We will never come to know it is missing.

How to Overcome these drawback:

- Interact with customers, business analysis, and developers closely.
- If you have better domain knowledge. Number of mistakes will be reduced.

Ex: ATM – product knowledge

Banking – Domain knowledge

- Based on the knowledge of products which are already released in the market.

When we do Exploratory Testing:

- Whenever a requirement is not there.
- Requirement is there, we are not able to understand it.
- Requirements are there, we are able to understand it but don't have time to go through it.

How do we manage Exploratory testing projects?

Understanding the Requirements

Documented & Tested: Based on documentation, TE analyzes the software and tests it and also identifies new features and documents it and tests it.

Regression Testing:

Testing the unchanged features to make sure that it is not broken because of the changes (changes means – addition, modification, deletion or defect fixing

Re-execution of same test cases in different builds or releases to make sure that changes (addition, modification, deletion or defect fixing) are not introducing defects in unchanged features.

When the development team gives a build, chances are there they would have done some changes. That change might affect unchanged features. So, Testing the unchanged features to make sure that it is not broken because of the changes is called Regression Testing.

Majority of time spent in testing is on regression testing

Example of Regression Testing:

Let's Consider 1st build – Customer gives requirements – development team start developing features – testing team start writing test cases – testing team write about 1000 test cases for the 1st release of the product and after execution of the test cases – the product is released – customer does acceptance testing – and the product is moved to production.

2nd build – now, customer asks for Two extra features to be added and gives the requirements for the extra features – development team start building the extra features – testing team start writing test cases for the extra features – about 200 extra test cases are written – thus a total of 1200 test cases are written for both the releases – now testing team – start testing the new features using the 200 new test cases – once that's done, then start testing the old features using the old 1000 test cases to check if adding new features has broken the old features. Testing old features is called regression testing. Once everything has been tested, now the product is given to the customer who does acceptance testing and then moves the product to production.

3rd build – after the 2nd release, the customer wants to remove one of the features (say Loans) – he removes all the Loans related test cases (about 100) – and then tests all the other features to check if all the other features are working fine. This is called regression testing.

Types of Regression Testing:

- Unit Regression Testing
- Regional Regression Testing
- Full Regression Testing

Unit Regression Testing:

Here, we are going to test only the changes.

In Build B01, a bug is found and a report is sent to the developer. The developer fixes the bug and also sends along some new features developed in the 2nd build B02. The TE tests only if the bug is fixed.

For ex,

When the developer gives the above application for testing in the 1st build – the TE finds that clicking on the submit button goes to a blank page – this is a bug and is sent to the developer for defect fixing – when the new build comes in along with the defect fixes – the TE tests only the submit button. Here we are not going to test the other features of the 1st build and move to test the new features sent in the 2nd build. We are sure that fixing the submit button is not going to affect other features – so we test only the fixed defect.

Testing only the modified features is called Unit Regression Testing.

Let us consider another example,

Build 1 – B01 Build 2 – B02

CREATE USER

Name

Address

Telephone Number

Email Id

….

....

....

....

SUBMIT

CANCEL

(Search field) 1 – 20 characters

SEARCH

CANCEL

(Search field) 1 – 40 characters

SEARCH

CANCEL

For the above application, in the 1st build – the developers develop a "search" field which accepts 1-20 characters. The TE tests the search field using test case design techniques.

Now, the customer makes some changes in the requirements and requests that the "search" field be able to accept 1-40 characters. The TE tests only the search field to see if it accepts 1-40 characters and doesn't test for any other feature of the 1st build.

b) Regional Regression Testing (RRT)

Testing the changes and impact regions is called Regional Regression Testing.

Build 1 – B01

Impact Areas Changes in B02

The module 1,2,3,4 is given by developers for testing during the 1st build. The TE finds a defect in Module 4. The defect report is sent to the developers and the development team fixes the bug and sends the 2nd build in which the bug is fixed. Now, the TE realizes that defect fixing in module 4 has impacted some features in module 1 and 3. So, the TE first tests module 4 where the bug has been fixed and then tests the impact areas i.e, module 1 and module 3. This is known as regional regression testing.

Story 1

After the 1st build, the customer sends some changes in requirements and also to add new features to be added to the product. The requirements are sent to both the development team and testing team.

The development team starts making the changes and also building the new features as per the requirements.

Now, the test lead sends a mail to the customer asking – which and all are the impact areas that will be affected after the necessary changes are made – so that he will get an idea as to which and all features needed to be tested again. He also sends a mail to the development team to know which and all areas in the application will be affected as a result of the modifications and additions of features. And similarly he sends a mail to his testing team for a list of impact areas. Thus he gathers impact list from the customer, development team and also the testing team.

This impact list is sent to all testing engineers who look at the list and check if their features are modified and if yes then they do regional regression testing. The impact areas and changed areas are all tested by the respective engineers for whom the features are allotted. Each

Module 1

Module 2

Module 3

Module 4

TE tests only his features which could have been affected as a result of the changes and modifications.

The problem with the above method is that the test lead may not get the full idea of the impact areas because the customer and development team may not have so much time to respond to his emails.

Story 2

To solve the above problem (story 1), we do the following.

Whenever a new build comes in along with new features and defect fixes. The testing team will have a standing meeting – they discuss if their features are affected by the above changes and thus they themselves do impact analysis and come up with the impact list where maximum possible impact areas are covered and chances of bugs creeping up is less.

Whenever the new build comes, the testing team does the following,

Smoke testing (check basic functionality)

Test new features

Test the modified features

Retesting the bugs

Regional regression testing (checking the impact areas)

The below graph shows that increase in testing effort will not lead to catching more bugs,

Thus, we can see that the initial effort spent on regional regression testing will lead to catching more bugs. But with the effort spent on full regression testing will diminish the number of bugs we catch. Thus, we can conclude an increase in testing effort will not lead to catching more bugs.

Full Regression Testing:

After 2 releases of the product, during the 3rd release – customer asks for adding 2 new features, deleting 1 feature and modifying 1 feature. Also some bugs needed to be fixed. The testing team after doing impact analysis find out that making all the above changes will lead to testing the entire product.

Thus, testing the changes and all the remaining features is called **Full Regression Testing**.

When do we do Full Regression Testing?

- When changes are more
- Whenever the changes are done in the root of the product. For example, JVM is the root of Java applications.
- Whenever any changes are made in JVM, the entire Java application is tested.

Regional Regression Testing is the most preferred method of regression testing. But the problem is, we may miss a lot of bugs doing Regional Regression Testing.

We can solve this problem by the following method – when a product is given for testing, for the 1st ten cycles, we do regional regression testing, then for the 11th cycle, we do FRT. Again, for the next 10 cycles, we do RRT and for the 21st cycle we do FRT. Thus we continue like this, for the last ten cycles of the release – we do only FRT. Thus, following the above method – we can catch a lot of bugs.

Performance Testing:

Testing the stability and response time of an application by applying load is called Performance Testing.

Response Time: Time taken to response in a cycle

Response Time = T1 + T2 + T3

T1 --> Time taken to send request

T2 --> Time taken to run request

T3 --> Time taken to response the request

T3 T1 & T3 -->Depends on network

Stability: Ability to withstand the design number of loads / users.

Load: Number of users.

Instances: Duplicate copies of programs.

Performance Tool: Load Runner

How to use the tool and perform performance testing?

When the Test Engineer uses the load runner to check performance of the program.

- Write the performance program in load runner and enter number of virtual users, click on RUN.
- The request goes to the application server and starts running, if it runs the
- software for Number of users (2, 00,000).
- Then the Load runner gives the result with the help of a graph.
- Whenever it is Time consumes, then we change the code and speed up the process.

Types of Performance Testing:

- Load Testing: Testing the stability and response time of an application by applying load is less than or equal to Number of users.
- Stress Testing: Testing the stability and response time of an application by applying load which is more than the design number of users.
- Volume Testing: Testing the stability and response time of an application when a huge volume of data is transferred through it.
- Soak Testing: Testing the stability and response time of an application by applying load continuously for a particular period of time.

i.e., Immerse the software in load.

GLOBALIZATION TESTING:

Developing the application for multiple languages is called globalization and testing the application which is developed for multiple languages is called globalization testing.

There are 2 types of globalization testing,

- Internationalization Testing (I18N testing)
- Localization Testing (L10N testing)

Internationalization Testing (I18N testing) is a process that ensures a software application or product is designed and developed in a way that makes it adaptable for various locales and languages without requiring engineering changes. Here's an overview of what internationalization testing involves, when it is conducted, and who typically performs it, along with an example:

What is Internationalization Testing (I18N Testing)?

- **Purpose**: Internationalization testing verifies that the software application can support multiple languages, cultural conventions, and regional settings without modification to the core codebase.
- **Focus**: It focuses on design and architecture aspects like encoding standards, date/time formats, currency symbols, text direction, and UI layout flexibility.
- **Goal**: Ensure that the application can be easily localized for different markets and regions.

When is Internationalization Testing Conducted?

- **Early Development Stages**: Internationalization testing starts during the initial phases of software development, ideally alongside functional testing.
- **Throughout Development**: It continues throughout the development lifecycle to validate that internationalization considerations are integrated into every feature and module.
- **Before Localization**: It is essential to complete internationalization testing before localization (translation of text and adaptation to local cultures), as internationalization ensures the software is ready for localization.

Who Performs Internationalization Testing?

- **Testers and QA Engineers**: Specialized testers with knowledge of internationalization standards, localization practices, and experience in testing software for global markets.
- **Localization Experts**: They collaborate with the development team to ensure that the application's design and architecture support easy adaptation to different languages and cultural norms.
- **Developers**: They play a crucial role in implementing internationalization best practices as identified during testing.

Example Scenario:

Scenario: A software company is developing a new e-commerce platform that aims to be used globally. They want to ensure the platform can handle multiple languages, currencies, and cultural preferences.

- **What**: Internationalization testing involves verifying that the e-commerce platform:
  - Supports Unicode character encoding to display text in different languages (e.g., English, Spanish, Chinese).
  - Adapts date and time formats based on the user's locale preferences (e.g., MM/DD/YYYY vs DD/MM/YYYY).
  - Displays currency symbols correctly and handles currency conversion accurately.
  - Allows for flexible UI layouts to accommodate text expansion or contraction when translated into different languages.

- **When**: Internationalization testing is conducted throughout the development process, starting from the initial design phases to ensure internationalization considerations are embedded in the architecture and continue through iterative development cycles.
- **Who**: Testers with expertise in internationalization standards, localization engineers, and developers work together to identify and resolve internationalization issues early in the development process.

Summary:

Internationalization testing is critical for ensuring that software applications are designed to be adaptable and culturally appropriate for global markets. By conducting thorough internationalization testing, organizations can streamline the localization process and provide a seamless user experience across different languages and regions.

Localization testing ensures that a software application or product has been adapted for a specific locale or target market, including language, cultural conventions, and regional preferences. Here's an overview of what localization testing involves, why it is important, and who typically performs it, along with an example:

What is Localization Testing?

- **Purpose**: Localization testing verifies that the software application functions correctly and meets the linguistic, cultural, and regulatory requirements of a specific target market or locale.

- **Focus**: It includes testing localized content, such as translated text, date/time formats, currency symbols, images, and UI elements to ensure they are accurate and appropriate for the target audience.

- **Goal**: Ensure the software is culturally and linguistically suitable for users in different regions.

Why is Localization Testing Important?

- **User Experience**: Provides a localized user interface (UI) that enhances usability and makes the software more accessible to users in different countries.

- **Compliance**: Ensures compliance with local regulations and standards regarding language usage, data formats, and other cultural considerations.

- **Market Expansion**: Facilitates market expansion by adapting the software to meet the needs and expectations of users in diverse geographical regions.

Who Performs Localization Testing?

- **Localization Testers**: Specialists with expertise in linguistics, cultural nuances, and the ability to test the software in different languages and locales.

- **Localization Engineers**: They manage the technical aspects of the localization process, including integrating translated content, adjusting UI elements, and ensuring consistency across different language versions.

- **Testers and QA Engineers**: Collaborate with localization experts to validate the functionality and usability of the localized software.

Example Scenario:

Scenario: A software company is preparing to launch a mobile application for online food delivery services in multiple countries. They have completed internationalization testing to ensure the application can support different languages and cultural conventions. Now, they need to perform localization testing to ensure the application is fully adapted for specific target markets.

- **What**: Localization testing involves:

  - Verifying the accuracy and quality of translated text in the UI, including menus, buttons, error messages, and instructions.

  - Testing date and time formats to ensure they conform to local conventions (e.g., MM/DD/YYYY vs DD/MM/YYYY).

  - Checking currency symbols and formats to ensure they are displayed correctly and match local currency preferences.

  - Testing localized images, graphics, and multimedia content to ensure they are culturally appropriate and relevant.

  - Verifying compliance with local regulations and standards related to data privacy, language usage, and content presentation.

- **Why**: Localization testing is crucial to ensure the application meets the linguistic and cultural expectations of users in each target market, enhancing user satisfaction and adoption.

- **Who**: Localization testers, along with QA engineers and developers, collaborate to perform thorough testing across different language versions and locales, ensuring the application's readiness for global deployment.

Summary:

Localization testing ensures that software applications are adapted and localized effectively for specific target markets, enhancing usability, compliance, and user satisfaction. By conducting comprehensive localization testing, organizations can ensure their software meets the diverse needs and preferences of users worldwide.

- **Defect,Defect Tracking and Defect Life Cycle**

Defect : If a feature is not working according to the requirement, it is called a **defect**.

Deviation from requirement specification is called a defect.

Why do we get Defect?

A bug occurs only because of the following reasons,

- Wrong implementation:- Here, wrong implementation means coding. For example, in an application – when you click on the "SALES" link – it goes to the "PURCHASE" page – this occurs because of wrong coding. Thus, this is a bug.
- Missing implementation:- We may not have developed the code only for that feature. For example, opening the application – "SALES" link is not there only – that means the feature has not been developed only – this is a bug.
- Extra implementation:- The developer develops extra features which are not needed and not there in the requirements also. For ex, consider the below application
- **What is the difference b/w defect, bug, error and failure?**

BUG is the informal name given to the defect.

ERROR – it is a mistake done in the program because of which we are not able to compile or run the program

FAILURE – defect leads to failure or defect causes failure. Chances are there 1 defect might lead to 1 failure or multiple failures.

Take the example of the Amount Transfer feature not working for end users when the end user tries to transfer money – the submit button is not working. Thus, this is a failure.

DEFECT – The variation between the actual results and expected results is known as defect

Developer develops the product – the test engineer starts testing the product – he finds a defect – now the TE must send the defect to the development team.

He prepares a defect report – and sends a mail to the Development lead saying "bug open".

Development lead looks at the mail and at the bug – and by looking at the bug – he comes to know which development engineer developed that feature which had a bug – and sends the defect report to that particular developer and says "bug assigned".

The development engineer fixes the bug – and sends a mail to the test engineer saying "bug fixed" – he also "cc mail" to the development lead.

Now the TE takes the new build in which the bug is fixed – and if the bug is really fixed – then sends a mail to the developer saying "bug closed" and also "cc mail" to the development lead.

Every bug will have a unique number.

If the defect is still there – it will be sent back as "bug reopen".

We should also send a copy of the defect report to the TL. Why do we do this? Because

- He should be aware of all the issues that are there in the project
- To get visibility (i.e, he should know that we are working)

90% of projects – we don't take permission from Test Lead to send bugs to development team.

Around 10% of projects, we take permission because,

- Customer is new – for ex, A has a testing team which is testing a product developed by Vodafone developers. We can't send all sorts of major, minor and critical bugs to their development team. So the test lead first approves the defect and then sends it to the development team saying it's a valid bug.
- When we are new to the project

When should we send defects to the development team? – As soon as we catch the defect, we send it to the development team.

Why do we send it immediately?

- Otherwise someone else will send the defect (common features)
- Development team will have sufficient time to fix the bug if we send the bug ASAP.

Customer gives requirements – developers are developing the s/w – testing team is writing test cases looking at the requirements

Developer develops the product – the test engineer starts testing the product – he finds a defect – now the TE must send the defect to the development team.

He prepares a defect report – and sends a mail to the Development lead saying "**bug open**".

Development lead looks at the mail and at the bug – and by looking at the bug – he comes to know which development engineer developed that feature which had a bug – and sends the defect report to that particular developer and says "**bug assigned**".

The development engineer fixes the bug – and sends a mail to the test engineer saying "**bug fixed**" – he also "cc mail" to the development lead.

Now the TE takes the new build in which the bug is fixed and re-tests it again – and if the bug is really fixed – then sends a mail to the developer saying "**bug closed**" and also "cc mail" to the development lead.

Every bug will have a unique number.

If the defect is still there – it will be sent back as "**bug reopen**".

- CLOSED
- RE-OPEN
- FIXED
- ASSIGNED
- OPEN
- REJECT / Not a defect
- DUPLICATE
- Cannot be fixed
- Not Reproducible
- Postponed / Fixed in future release
- RFE – Request for enhancement

"REJECT" BUG:

Now, when the TE sends a defect report – the Development Lead will look at it and reject the bug.

Bug is rejected because,

1) Misunderstanding of requirements

2) While installing or configuring the product – wrongly configured or installed the product and we found a bug in the product – send it to development team – developer says "reject" because he looks at the defect report and comes to know that the Testing team has not installed the product correctly.

3) Referring to old requirements

Chances are there that the Testing team may be referring to old requirements while testing the product.

For ex, - in the 1st build – developers have given the product for testing in which a sales link button is there, test engineer does testing and reports any defects – in the 2nd build, customer has given a requirement change to the development team where-in he has asked them to remove the sales link button – but the testing team is not aware of this change – so when the development team gives the new build – obviously they would have removed the sales button – test engineer when he looks at the feature – he is referring to old requirements which has sales link button – but in the new requirements it has been removed which the test engineer is not aware of – so he reports a bug – development team then reply back saying "refer to new requirements in which sales link button has been removed".

4) Because of extra features

"DUPLICATE" BUG:

The TE finds a bug and sends a defect report and also assigns the bug report a number – let's say he sends a bug report numbered as Bug 25 – now the developer replies back by saying "Bug 25 is duplicate of Bug 10" i.e, another Test engineer has already sent that bug earlier and it is being fixed.

Why do we get duplicate bugs?

- Because of common features – Lets say Test Engineer A and B are testing an application – Test Engineer A and B to test their features must Login to the application using valid username and password before they can go deep into the application and start testing their features – A enters valid username and password and clicks on Login button – it goes to a blank page – this is a bug – so A prepares a defect report for this bug and sends it to developer – After sometime, B also tries to login and finds the same bug – he also prepares a defect report and sends it to developer – but developer sends back defect report of B saying "it is a duplicate".
- B finds bug in A's module – let's say A and B are testing their respective features – A is doing functional testing and integration testing on all his features – Similarly B is also testing all his features – In one scenario, B needs to go to A's feature(say m12) and send data to B's feature(say m23) – when B clicks on m12, he finds a bug – although its feature of A, he can still prepare a defect report and send it to developers – and B sends the defect report to development team – now, A after testing all his features comes to his feature m12 – he also

finds the same defect and sends a defect report – but the developers send it back saying "it is duplicate".

CANNOT BE FIXED:

Chances are there – Test Engineer finds a bug and sends it to Development Lead – development lead looks at the bug and sends it back saying "**cannot be fixed**".

Why does this happen? – Because,

• Technology itself is not supporting i.e, programming language we are using itself is not having capability to solve the problem

• Whenever there is a bug in the root of the product. If it's a minor bug, then development lead says "cannot be fixed". But, if it's a critical bug, then development lead cannot reject the bug

• If the cost of fixing the bug is more than the cost of the bug itself – cost of the bug means loss incurred because of the bug.

POSTPONED or Fixed in the next release:

a) We find a bug during the end of the release (could be major or minor but cannot be critical) – developers won't have time to fix the bug – such a bug will be postponed and fixed in the next release and the bug status will be "open".

b) Developers have built the above application – Test Engineers are testing the application and they find a bug – now, the bug is sent to the development team. Development team looks at the report – and replies back to the testing team saying "they will not fix the bug for now, as the customer is thinking of making some changes to that module or he might as well ask for a requirement change where-in the module itself might have to be removed" – so they won't fix the bug for now – but if no requirement change happens, then they will fix the bug.

c) If the bug is minor and it is in a feature exposed to internal users.

For ex, Consider Citibank employee using a s/w where-in he is making keeping track of accounts and customer details – now, for example if the "Sort by name" feature is not working – it's ok because it's a minor bug because the development team can always fix the bug during the next release.

NOT REPRODUCIBLE:

Open the application in Mozilla FireFox

Let us consider the above application – the TE is testing the above application in Mozilla Firefox– when he clicks on the SALES link button – it goes to a blank page – this is a bug – the TE prepares a defect report and sends it to the development team.

….

…..

…..

……

…….

…

….

…..

SALES

……

…

…

….

…..

BLANK PAGE

1) Open browser and enter www.citibank.com and click on Go button

2) Login using valid username and password

3) In the homepage, click on "SALES link button"

4) It goes to blank page

Open the application in Internet Explorer

The development lead looks at the defect report and opens the application in Internet Explorer – when he clicks on the Sales link button, the Sales page opens and the application works perfectly.

Then, what was the problem? – the answer is, the TE didn't specify in the defect report in which browser to open the application – so, the application didn't work for the TE in Mozilla FireFox – but, when the developer opened it in Internet Explorer, the application worked totally fine.

Since the developer is not able to see any defect – he replies back by saying "I am not able to find the defect" or "I am not able to reproduce the defect".

Why do we get "not reproducible" defects?

1. Because of platform mismatch

2. Because of improper defect report

3. Because of data mismatch

4. Because of build mismatch

5. Because of inconsistent defects

1) Because of platform mismatch

- Because of OS mismatch
- Because of browser mismatch
- Because of 'version of browser' mismatch
- Because of 'settings of version' mismatch

2) Because of improper defect report

In the given application – TE is testing the application – when he enters all the user details and selects checkbox and clicks on Submit button – it goes to blank page – but, when the TE does not select the checkbox and clicks on Submit

….

….

…..

..

…

….

….

….

….

SALES

…

…

…

SALES

…

…..

...

......

....

.....

....

....

.....

button, a new user account is created, i.e, it works fine. The TE prepares a defect report and sends it to the development lead.

The Dev team looks at the report(as shown in box) – and tests the application – it is working absolutely fine.

Then what happened? – Observe the defect report sent by the testing team – nowhere as he mentioned to "select checkbox and click on submit button" – thus because of the improper defect report – the development team is not able to reproduce the defect.

3) Because of data mismatch

Consider the example shown below,

USER DETAILS

....

....

...

...

....

...

...

REMEMBER PASSWORD

....

....

....

....

....

....

SUBMIT

CANCEL

1) Open browser and enter www.citibank.com and click on Go button

2) Enter user details and click on Submit button

3) It goes to blank page

INBOX (102 mails)

...

...

...

...

...

...

...

BLANK PAGE

Login as ABC and click on Inbox in homepage of ABC

The above email application has been developed – the TE starts testing the above application – after testing and testing the above application using username ABC and valid password – there are almost 101 mails in ABC's inbox – now, again when the TE opens the application and goes to test the application – no mails are being displayed when he clicks in Inbox and instead he gets a blank page. So – the defect he has found is that – when the number of mails in Inbox exceeds 100 mails, he gets a blank page – so he prepares a defect report as shown in the box below,

The development team looks at the defect report – he logs in to the application using username XYZ and clicks on Inbox – no blank page is displayed and the Inbox is working fine.

What happened here? – The TE should have mentioned in the defect report as "Login as ABC" or "Login to any mailbox which has more than 100 mails". Thus, the developer does not find any defects and thus he mentions it as "not reproducible defect".

4) Because of build mismatch:

Developer develops build 1 and gives it for testing – in Build 1, there are 2 defects – bug 1 and bug 2 – TE while testing finds bug1 and reports it to development team – development team when they fix bug1, bug2 automatically gets fixed – development team is developing build 2 and gives it to testing team for testing – testing team just when it finishes testing build1 – he finds Bug 2 and reports it to

1) Open the browser and enter the following URL www.email.com

2) Login using valid username and password

3) Click on Inbox

4) Blank page is displayed

BUG 1

BUG 2

development team – the development team however do not find any defect as

they are testing build 2 – so they report back saying "bug is not reproducible".

4) Because of inconsistent defects

To explain this, let us consider an example : When TE is testing an email

application – he composes mail in User A and sends it to User B – he then logs

out from user A and logs into User B and checks B's inbox – but no mail is there

in the Inbox – thus he finds a defect – now, just to confirm the defect before

sending a defect report – the TE again logs into User A and sends a mail to User

B – he then logs out from User A and logs into User B and checks B's inbox –

but, this time the mail is there in B's inbox!!

Thus, we don't know when the defect comes and when the feature works fine.

This is called an inconsistent defect.

REQUEST FOR ENHANCEMENT (RFE)

Test engineer finds a bug and sends it to development team – when development

team look at the report sent by the TE – They know it's a bug, but they say its not a bug because its not part of the requirements.

Let us consider the example shown below,

In the above example, the TE is testing the above fields. After he enters all the data into the required fields, he realizes that he needs to clear all the data – but there is no CLEAR button – and he has to manually clear all the fields. He reports this as a bug – but the development team will look at the defect report and see that clear button is not mentioned in the requirements – so they don't reject or close the bug – instead they reply back to the Test Engineer saying that it is RFE. Developers agree that it is a bug – but will say that the customer have not specified these details and hence will give it a name as RFE.

CREATE USER

….

SUBMIT

CREATE USER

…

…

…

…

…

…

…

…

…

… CANCEL

If a defect is known as RFE, then we can bill the customer. Otherwise, development team needs to fix the bug

Development teams always have a tendency to call a defect as RFE, so a TE needs to check the justification given by development team – if it is valid, then he will accept it as a RFE – but if it is not, then he will respond to the development team with proper justification.

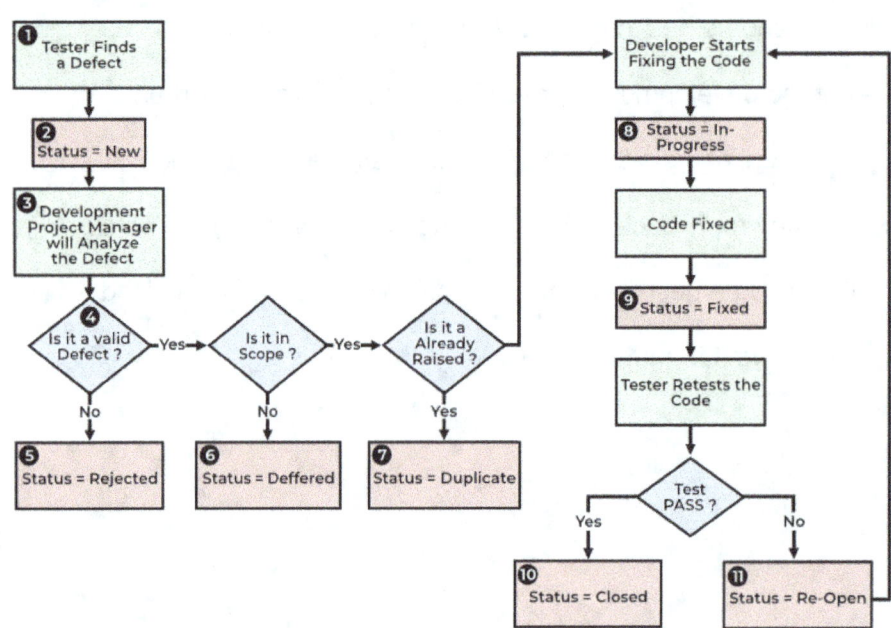

Defect Report:

Defect ID – it is a unique number given to the defect

Test Case Name – whenever we find a defect, we send the defect report and not the test case to the developer. For defect tracking, we only track the defect report and not the test case. Test case is only for reference for the TE. We always only send the defect report whenever we catch a bug.

When we are doing ad-hoc testing – no test case is written for ad-hoc testing because they are "out of the box" testing scenarios – if we find a critical bug – then we convert that ad-hoc scenario into a test case and send it to the development team.

Given below is – how a defect report looks like – it is a MS – WORD file.

DEFECT ID : BugID _ 1578

RELEASE NAME : Tiger

BUILD ID : B03

MODULE NAME : Sent Items

STATUS : Open

Assigned

Fixed

Closed

Duplicate

… etc etc

SEVERITY : Blocker OR Showstopper

Critical

Major

Minor

PRIORITY : High P1

Medium P2

Low P3

P4

TEST DATA : username = abc123 , password = xyz123

TEST ENVIRONMENT : In Windows XP, Internet Explorer 7.0

TEST CASE NAME : Yahoo _ SI _ mail list

FOUND BY :

BRIEF DESCRIPTION : Sent mails are not there in the Sent Items page

DETAILED DESCRIPTION : Following are the steps to reproduce the defect

1. Open the browser and enter the test URL

2. Login with valid username and password

3. Click on "compose" link

4. Enter valid data into all fields and click on Submit button

5. Click on Sent Items link

EXPECTED RESULT : Sent mail should be listed in Sent Items page

ACTUAL RESULT : Sent mail is not there in the Sent Items page

Screenshot of the Defect Circle the defect in the screenshot in red by using light shot tool.

How to track a defect manually?

1) Find a defect

2) Ensure that it is not duplicate (i.e, verify it in Defect Repository)

3) Prepare defect report

4) Store it in defect repository

5) Send it to development team

6) Manage defect life cycle (i.e, keep updating the status)

Tracking of defects using Automation (i.e, Defect Tracking Tool)

The various tools available are,

- Bugzilla
- Mantis
- Rational Clear Quest
- TeleLogic
- Bug_track
- QC – Quality Center – it is a test management tool – a part of it is used to track the defects.

SEVERITY of a Bug;

Severity is the impact of the bug on a customer's business.

- **Critical** – A major issue where a large piece of functionality or major system component is completely broken. There is no work around & testing cannot continue.
- **Major** – A major issue where a large piece of functionality or major system component is not working properly. There is a work around, however & testing can continue.
- **Minor** – A minor issue that imposes some loss of functionality, but for which there is an acceptable & easily reproducible workaround. Testing can proceed without interruption.

Blocker Defect:

There are 2 types in blocker defect,

- **Major flow is not working** – Login or signup itself is not working in CitiBank application
- **Major feature is not working** – Login to CitiBank. Amount Transfer is not working

PRIORITY of a Bug:

It is important to fix the bug (OR) how soon the defect should be fixed (OR) which are the defects to be fixed first.

- **High** – This has a major impact on the customer. This must be fixed immediately.
- **Medium** – This has a major impact on the customer. The problem should be fixed before release of the current version in development
- **Low** – This has a minor impact on the customer. The flow should be fixed if there is time, but it can be deferred with the next release.

Development team will fix the high priority defects first rather than of high severity.

Generally, severity is assigned by Tester / Test Lead & priority is assigned by Developer/Team Lead/Project Lead.

SDLC (Software Development Life Cycle):

It is a **step by step procedure to develop the software.**

It is a process of creating or altering systems and the models and methodologies that people use to develop these systems.

Any SDLC should result in a high quality system that meets or exceeds customer expectations, reaches completion within time and cost estimates, works effectively and efficiently and is inexpensive to maintain and cost effective to enhance.

Stages of Software Development life cycle:

- Requirement Collection
- Feasibility study
- Design
- Coding
- Testing
- Installation
- Maintenance

Stage 1	Stage 2	Stage 3	Stage 4	Stage 5	Stage 6
Planning & Requirement Analysis	Defining Requirements	Design	Development	Testing	Deployment & Maintenace
Planning	Defining	Design	Development	System Testing	Deployment and Maintenace
Define Project Scope	Functional Requirement	HLD	Coding Standard	Manual Testing	Release Planning
Set Objectives and Goals	Technical Requirement	LLD	Scalable Code	Automated Testing	Deployment Automation
Resource Planning	Requirement Reviews & Approved		Version Control		Maintenance
			Code Review		Feedback

6 Stages of Software Development Life Cycle

Types of Software Development life cycle:

- Waterfall Model
- Spiral Model
- Verification and Validation Model
- Prototype Model
- Hybrid Model
- Agile Model

Waterfall Model:

It is a traditional model

It is a sequential design process, often used in SDLC, in which the progress is seen as flowing steadily downwards (like a waterfall), through the different phases as shown in the figure,

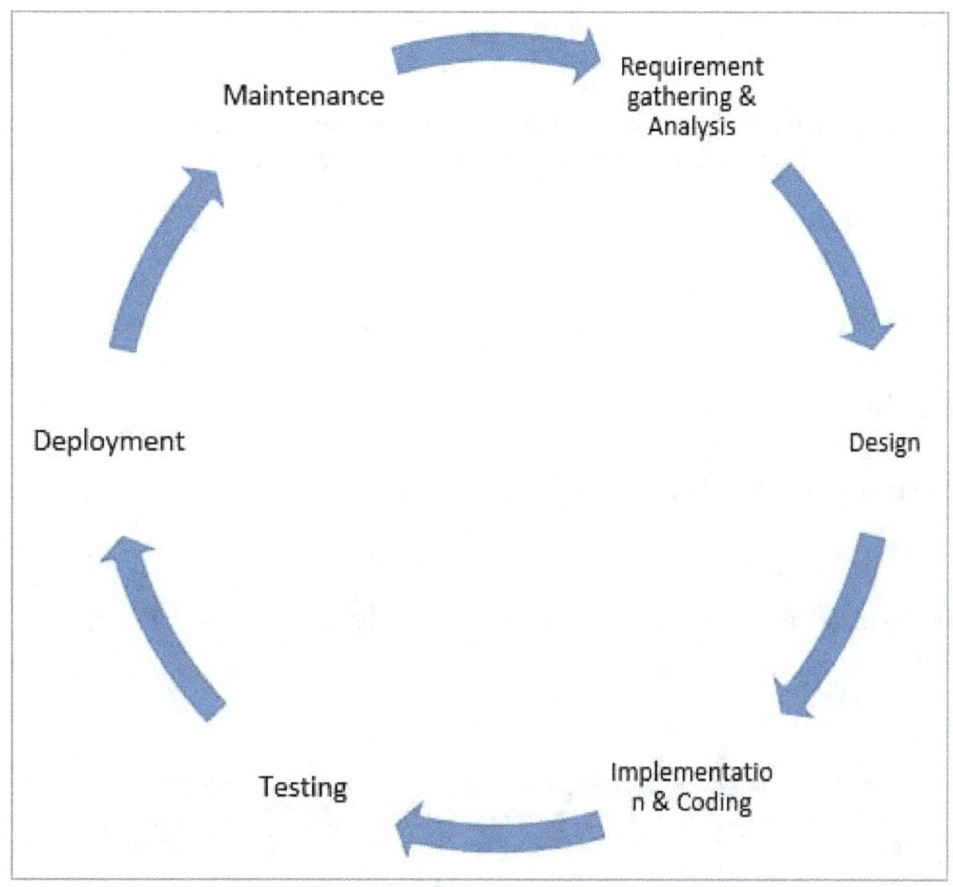

Requirements Collection:

Done by Business Analysts and Product Analysts

- Gathering requirements

- translates business language into software language

Feasibility Study:

Done by software team consisting of project managers, business analysts, architects, finance, HR, developers but not testers

- Here they decide whether the product can be developed and if yes, then which technology is best suited to develop it.

- Here we check for technical feasibility, financial feasibility, resource feasibility.

Design:

There are 2 stages in design,

High Level Design – gives the architecture of the software product to be developed and is done by architects and senior developers

Low Level Design – done by senior developers. It describes how each and every feature in the product should work and how every component should work. Here, only the design will be there and not the code.

Coding / Programming:

Done by all developers. This is the process where we start building the software and start writing the code for the product.

Testing:

Done by test engineers. It is the process of checking for all defects and rectifying them.

Installation:

Done by installation engineers. To install the product at a client's place for using after the software has been developed and tested.

Maintenance:

Here as the customer uses the product, he finds certain bugs and defects and sends the product back for error correction and bug fixing. Minor changes like adding, deleting or modifying any small feature in the software product.

Advantages of waterfall Model:

- It is Simple to adopt.
- Since Requirements are freezed , at the end we will get high quality products.

Disadvantages of waterfall Model:

- Total Investment is high.
- Not flexible because Testing starts after coding itself. Hence Requirement and Design is not tested, if there is a bug in those two stages, it will flow till the end and it leads to a lot of rework.

Applications:

- Whenever we are building a simple product / small application.
- For short term projects.

V – MODEL / V & V MODEL (Verification and Validation Model):

This model came up in order to overcome the drawback of waterfall model – here testing starts from the requirement stage itself.

The V & V model is shown in the figure in the next page.

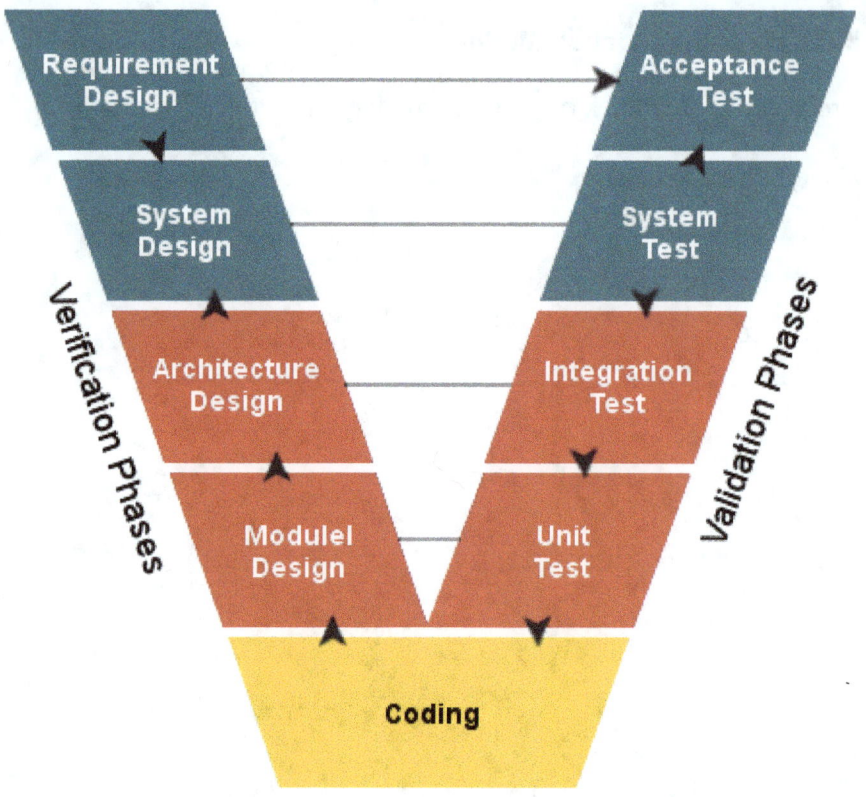

1) In the first stage, the client send the CRS both to developers and testers. The developers translate the CRS to the SRS.

The testers do the following tests on CRS,

1. Review CRS

a. Conflicts in the requirements

b. Missing requirements

c. Wrong requirements

2. Write Acceptance Test plan

3. Write Acceptance Test cases

The testing team reviews the CRS and identifies mistakes and defects and sends it to the development team for correcting the bugs. The development updates the CRS and continues developing SRS simultaneously.

2) In the next stage, the SRS is sent to the testing team for review and the developers start building the HLD of the product. The testers do the following tests on SRS,

1. Review SRS against CRS

a. Every CRS is converted to SRS

b. CRS not converted properly to SRS

2. Write System Test plan

3. Write System Test case

The testing team reviews every detail of the SRS if the CRS has been converted properly to SRS.

3) In the next stage, the developers start building the LLD of the product. The testers do the following tests on HLD,

1. Review HLD

2. Write Integration test plan

3. Write Integration test case

4) In the next stage, the developers start with the coding of the product. The testing team carries out the following tasks,

1. Review LLD

2. Write Functional test plan

3. Write Functional Test case

After coding, the developers themselves carry out unit testing or also known as white box testing. Here the developers check each and every line of code and if the code is correct. After white-box testing, the s/w product is sent to the testing team which tests the s/w product and carries out functional testing, integration testing, system testing and acceptance testing and finally delivers the product to the client.

How to handle requirement changes in V&V:

Whenever there is change in requirement, the same procedure continues and the documents will be updated.

Advantages of V&V model:

1) Testing starts in very early stages of product development which avoids downward flow of defects which in turn reduces lot of rework

2) Testing is involved in every stage of product development

3) Deliverables are parallel/simultaneous – as developers are building SRS, testers are testing CRS and also writing ATP and ATC and so on. Thus as the developers give the finished product to testing team, the testing team is ready with all the test plans and test cases and thus the project is completed fast.

4) Total investment is less – as there is no downward flow of defects. Thus there is less or no re-work

Drawbacks of V&V model:

1) Initial investment is more – because right from the beginning testing team is needed

2) More documentation work – because of the test plans and test cases and all other documents

Applications of V&V model

We go for V&V model in the following cases,

1) For long term projects

2) For complex applications

3) When a customer is expecting a very high quality product within a stipulated time frame because every stage is tested and developers & testing team are working in parallel.

Agile methodology:

- Agile methodology which is used to develop a software
- Agile is incremental and iterative
- In Agile we develop the software in multiple stages
- Incremental-Which we are adding the model ,Iterative- Same process again and again Collecting the requirement, Design, developing, Testing then giving the software to developers, This process is repeatedly called as iterative.
- Where the requirement keeps on changing as a company we should be flexible in handling these requirements changes, developing those requirements changes, developing those requirement changes ,testing those given requirement changes and finally giving the working piece of the software to the customer within the time.

Advantages of agile methodology:

- Frequent delivery
- Face to Face communication with client every week and requirement changes are allowed in any stages of the development

Disadvantages of agile methodology:

- Less Documentation
- Maintenance problem

Scrum Team:

It is a group of people involved in developing stories.

Scrum Team contains two different teams

- Core Team
- shared Team

1. **Core Team**

    Core team contains scrum master development team and testing team

2. **Shared Team**

    Shared team contains business analyst, architect, UX/UI designer, Database designer, product owner.

Product Backlog:

It is a document which prioritizes List of stories.

Daily standup meeting

It is a meeting which is conducted every day in the morning. Here the entire scrum team meets together and discuss about various things

- What were the tasks that were performed yesterday?
- What are the problems that engineers have faced yesterday to complete the task?
- What are the tasks that they are planning to do today?
- What are the problems that might be faced today?

    Everyday the daily standup will be conducted for 10 -20 min.

    We conduct this to improve the efficiency of the engineer's.

In Agile methodologies, particularly in frameworks like Scrum, an Impediment Backlog refers to a list or collection of obstacles, blockers, or issues that are hindering the progress of the team. Here's a more detailed explanation:

What is an Impediment?

An impediment in Agile terms is anything that slows down or prevents a Scrum team from achieving its goals during a Sprint or impedes their overall progress. These can be issues such as:

- **External Dependencies**: Dependencies on teams or resources outside the control of the Scrum team.
- **Lack of Skills or Resources**: Missing skills or resources needed to complete a task or user story.
- **Technical Issues**: Problems with tools, infrastructure, or technology.
- **Communication Issues**: Misunderstandings or lack of communication within the team or with stakeholders.
- **Organizational Barriers**: Policies, procedures, or organizational structures that hinder progress.

Impediment Backlog

The Impediment Backlog is a structured list where the Scrum team records and tracks these impediments. It serves several purposes:

1. **Visibility**: It makes impediments visible to everyone involved in the project, including the Scrum team, Product Owner, and stakeholders.
2. **Prioritization**: Impediments are prioritized based on their impact on the team's ability to deliver value. This helps the team focus on resolving the most critical impediments first.
3. **Tracking and Resolution**: Each impediment in the backlog is actively managed and tracked. The Scrum Master or the team takes ownership of resolving impediments by removing them or minimizing their impact.
4. **Continuous Improvement**: Managing impediments encourages a culture of continuous improvement within the team and the organization. By systematically addressing issues that slow down progress, teams can become more efficient and effective over time.

Handling Impediments

- **Daily Standup**: Teams often discuss impediments during the daily standup meeting to bring visibility and seek help in resolving them.
- **Scrum Master Role**: The Scrum Master plays a crucial role in facilitating the removal of impediments. They may work with the team, Product Owner, and stakeholders to eliminate barriers to progress.
- **Retrospective**: The Sprint Retrospective is an opportunity for the team to reflect on what went well and what could be improved, including addressing any recurring or significant impediments

StoryBoard/White Board:

- Storyboard will be generally hanged where people rome around
- This board contains assigned tasks, ongoing tasks, completed tasks
- Storyboard is created to improve the efficiency of the engineer's
- This board will be maintained by scrum master.

Burn-down chart:

- It is a graph which represents work left out vs time
- This graph will be prepared by the scrum master
- This graph is created to check whether the engineer's are reaching the story point or not.

Sprint:

A Sprint is a time-boxed iteration of work in Scrum, usually lasting between one to four weeks. During a Sprint, a cross-functional team works collaboratively to deliver a potentially shippable product increment. The scope of work is determined at the beginning of the Sprint and should not be changed during the Sprint, ensuring focus and commitment.

Sprint Backlog:

The Sprint Backlog is a list of tasks or user stories that the Scrum team commits to completing during the Sprint. It is derived from the Product Backlog items selected for the Sprint, broken down into smaller tasks, and estimated for effort. The Sprint Backlog evolves as tasks are completed, new insights are gained, and priorities change

Velocity:

Velocity is a measure of the amount of work a Scrum team can complete in a Sprint, based on past performance. It is usually expressed in story points (or another agreed-upon unit of measure) and is calculated by summing up the story points of all user stories or tasks completed during a Sprint. Velocity helps teams forecast how much work they can realistically achieve in future Sprints and assists in planning and managing workload.

Chicken:

In Agile terminology, "chickens" refer to individuals who are involved with or have a stake in the project but are not directly part of the Scrum team. They might include stakeholders, managers, or other interested parties who attend Scrum events as observers but do not interfere with the team's work during a Sprint.

What is the Spiral Model?

The Spiral Model is a [Software Development Life Cycle (SDLC)](#) model that provides a systematic and iterative approach to software development. In its diagrammatic representation, it looks like a spiral with many loops. The exact number of loops of the spiral is unknown and can vary from project to project. Each loop of the spiral is called a **phase** of the software development process.

Some Key Points regarding the phase of a Spiral Model:

1. The exact number of phases needed to develop the product can be varied by the project manager depending upon the project risks.
2. As the project manager dynamically determines the number of phases, the project manager has an important role in developing a product using the spiral model.
3. It is based on the idea of a spiral, with each iteration of the spiral representing a complete software development cycle, from [requirements gathering](#) and analysis to design, implementation, testing, and maintenance.

What Are the Phases of the Spiral Model?

The Spiral Model is a risk-driven model, meaning that the focus is on managing risk through multiple iterations of the software development process. It consists of the following phases:

1. **Planning:** The first phase of the Spiral Model is the planning phase, where the scope of the project is determined and a plan is created for the next iteration of the spiral.
2. **Risk Analysis:** In the risk analysis phase, the risks associated with the project are identified and evaluated.
3. **Engineering:** In the engineering phase, the software is developed based on the requirements gathered in the previous iteration.
4. **Evaluation:** In the evaluation phase, the software is evaluated to determine if it meets the customer's requirements and if it is of high quality.

5. **Planning:** The next iteration of the spiral begins with a new planning phase, based on the results of the evaluation.

The Spiral Model is often used for complex and large software development projects, as it allows for a more flexible and adaptable approach to software development. It is also well-suited to projects with significant uncertainty or high levels of risk.

> The Radius of the spiral at any point represents the expenses (cost) of the project so far, and the angular dimension represents the progress made so far in the current phase.

Spiral Model

Each phase of the Spiral Model is divided into four quadrants as shown in the above figure. The functions of these four quadrants are discussed below:

1. **Objective determination and identify alternative solutions:** Requirements are gathered from the customers and the objectives are identified, elaborated, and analyzed at the start of every phase. Then alternative solutions possible for the phase are proposed in this quadrant.
2. **Identify and resolve Risks:** During the second quadrant, all the possible solutions are evaluated to select the best possible solution. Then the risks associated with that solution are identified and the risks are resolved using the best possible strategy. At the end of this quadrant, the Prototype is built for the best possible solution.
3. **Develop the next version of the Product:** During the third quadrant, the identified features are developed and verified through testing. At the end of the third quadrant, the next version of the software is available.
4. **Review and plan for the next Phase:** In the fourth quadrant, the Customers evaluate the so-far developed version of the software. In the end, planning for the next phase is started.

Risk Handling in Spiral Model

A risk is any adverse situation that might affect the successful completion of a software project. The most important feature of the spiral model is handling these unknown risks after the project has started. Such risk resolutions are easier done by developing a prototype.

1. The spiral model supports coping with risks by providing the scope to build a prototype at every phase of software development.
2. The Prototyping Model also supports risk handling, but the risks must be identified completely before the start of the development work of the project.
3. But in real life, project risk may occur after the development work starts, in that case, we cannot use the Prototyping Model.
4. In each phase of the Spiral Model, the features of the product dated and analyzed, and the risks at that point in time are identified and are resolved through prototyping.
5. Thus, this model is much more flexible compared to other SDLC models.

Why is the Spiral Model called Meta Model?

The Spiral model is called a Meta-Model because it subsumes all the other SDLC models. For example, a single loop spiral actually represents the Iterative Waterfall Model.

1. The spiral model incorporates the stepwise approach of the [Classical Waterfall Model](#).
2. The spiral model uses the approach of the [Prototyping Model](#) by building a prototype at the start of each phase as a risk-handling technique.
3. Also, the spiral model can be considered as supporting the [Evolutionary model](#) – the iterations along the spiral can be considered as evolutionary levels through which the complete system is built.

Advantages of the Spiral Model

Below are some advantages of the Spiral Model.

1. **Risk Handling:** The projects with many unknown risks that occur as the development proceeds, in that case, Spiral Model is the best development model to follow due to the risk analysis and risk handling at every phase.
2. **Good for large projects:** It is recommended to use the Spiral Model in large and complex projects.
3. **Flexibility in Requirements:** Change requests in the Requirements at a later phase can be incorporated accurately by using this model.
4. **Customer Satisfaction:** Customers can see the development of the product at the early phase of the software development and thus, they habituated with the system by using it before completion of the total product.
5. **Iterative and Incremental Approach:** The Spiral Model provides an iterative and incremental approach to software development, allowing for flexibility and adaptability in response to changing requirements or unexpected events.
6. **Emphasis on Risk Management:** The Spiral Model places a strong emphasis on risk management, which helps to minimize the impact of uncertainty and risk on the software development process.
7. **Improved Communication:** The Spiral Model provides for regular evaluations and reviews, which can improve communication between the customer and the development team.
8. **Improved Quality:** The Spiral Model allows for multiple iterations of the software development process, which can result in improved software quality and reliability.

Disadvantages of the Spiral Model

Below are some main disadvantages of the spiral model.

1. **Complex:** The Spiral Model is much more complex than other SDLC models.
2. **Expensive:** Spiral Model is not suitable for small projects as it is expensive.
3. **Too much dependability on Risk Analysis:** The successful completion of the project is very much dependent on Risk Analysis. Without very highly experienced experts, it is going to be a failure to develop a project using this model.
4. **Difficulty in time management:** As the number of phases is unknown at the start of the project, time estimation is very difficult.
5. **Complexity:** The Spiral Model can be complex, as it involves multiple iterations of the software development process.
6. **Time-Consuming:** The Spiral Model can be time-consuming, as it requires multiple evaluations and reviews.
7. **Resource Intensive:** The Spiral Model can be resource-intensive, as it requires a significant investment in planning, risk analysis, and evaluations.

The most serious issue we face in the cascade model is that it takes a long length to finish the item, and the product becomes obsolete. To tackle this issue, we have another methodology, which is known as the Winding model or spiral model. The winding model is otherwise called the cyclic model.

When To Use the Spiral Model?

1. When a project is vast in **software engineering,** a spiral model is utilized.
2. A spiral approach is utilized when frequent releases are necessary.
3. When it is appropriate to create a prototype
4. When evaluating risks and costs is crucial
5. The spiral approach is beneficial for projects with moderate to high risk.
6. The SDLC's spiral model is helpful when requirements are complicated and ambiguous.
7. If modifications are possible at any moment
8. When committing to a long-term project is impractical owing to shifting economic priorities.

Conclusion

Spiral Model is a valuable choice for software development projects where risk management is of high priority. Spiral Model delivers high-quality software by promoting risk identification, iterative development and continuous client feedback. When a project is vast in software engineering, a spiral model is utilized.

The Prototyping Model is one of the most popularly used **Software Development Life Cycle Models (SDLC models)**. This model is used when the customers do not know the exact project requirements beforehand. In this model, a prototype of the end product is first developed, tested, and refined as per customer feedback repeatedly till a final acceptable prototype is achieved which forms the basis for developing the final product.

Prototyping Model-Concept

In this process model, the system is partially implemented before or during the analysis phase thereby allowing the customers to see the product early in the life cycle. The process starts by interviewing the customers and developing the incomplete high-level paper model. This document is used to build the initial prototype supporting only the basic functionality as desired by the customer. Once the customer figures out the problems, the prototype is further refined to eliminate them. The process continues until the user approves the prototype and finds the working model to be satisfactory.

Steps of Prototyping Model

Step 1: Requirement Gathering and Analysis: This is the initial step in designing a prototype model. In this phase, users are asked about what they expect or what they want from the system.

Step 2: Quick Design: This is the second step in the Prototyping Model. This model covers the basic design of the requirement through which a quick overview can be easily described.

Step 3: Build a Prototype: This step helps in building an actual prototype from the knowledge gained from prototype design.

Step 4: Initial User Evaluation: This step describes the preliminary testing where the investigation of the performance model occurs, as the customer will tell the strengths and weaknesses of the design, which was sent to the developer.

Step 5: Refining Prototype: If any feedback is given by the user, then improving the client's response to feedback and suggestions, the final system is approved.

Step 6: Implement Product and Maintain: This is the final step in the phase of the Prototyping Model where the final system is tested and distributed to production, where the program is run regularly to prevent failures.

For more, you can refer to [Software Prototyping Model Phases](#).

Prototyping Model

Types of Prototyping Models

There are four types of Prototyping Models, which are described below.

- Rapid Throwaway Prototyping
- Evolutionary Prototyping
- Incremental Prototyping
- Extreme Prototyping

1. Rapid Throwaway Prototyping

- This technique offers a useful method of exploring ideas and getting customer feedback for each of them.
- In this method, a developed prototype need not necessarily be a part of the accepted prototype.
- Customer feedback helps prevent unnecessary design faults and hence, the final prototype developed is of better quality.

2. Evolutionary Prototyping

- In this method, the prototype developed initially is incrementally refined based on customer feedback till it finally gets accepted.
- In comparison to Rapid Throwaway Prototyping, it offers a better approach that saves time as well as effort.
- This is because developing a prototype from scratch for every iteration of the process can sometimes be very frustrating for the developers.

3. Incremental Prototyping

- In this type of incremental prototyping, the final expected product is broken into different small pieces of prototypes and developed individually.
- In the end, when all individual pieces are properly developed, then the different prototypes are collectively merged into a single final product in their predefined order.

- It's a very efficient approach that reduces the complexity of the development process, where the goal is divided into sub-parts and each sub-part is developed individually.
- The time interval between the project's beginning and final delivery is substantially reduced because all parts of the system are prototyped and tested simultaneously.
- Of course, there might be the possibility that the pieces just do not fit together due to some lack of ness in the development phase – this can only be fixed by careful and complete plotting of the entire system before prototyping starts.

4. Extreme Prototyping

This method is mainly used for web development. It consists of three sequential independent phases:

- In this phase, a basic prototype with all the existing static pages is presented in HTML format.
- In the 2nd phase, Functional screens are made with a simulated data process using a prototype services layer.
- This is the final step where all the services are implemented and associated with the final prototype.

This Extreme Prototyping method makes the project cycling and delivery robust and fast and keeps the entire developer team focused and centralized on product deliveries rather than discovering all possible needs and specifications and adding necessitated features.

Advantages of Prototyping Model

- The customers get to see the partial product early in the life cycle. This ensures a greater level of customer satisfaction and comfort.
- New requirements can be easily accommodated as there is scope for refinement.
- Missing functionalities can be easily figured out.
- Errors can be detected much earlier thereby saving a lot of effort and cost, besides enhancing the quality of the software.
- The developed prototype can be reused by the developer for more complicated projects in the future.
- Flexibility in design.
- Early feedback from customers and stakeholders can help guide the development process and ensure that the final product meets their needs and expectations.
- Prototyping can be used to test and validate design decisions, allowing for adjustments to be made before significant resources are invested in development.
- Prototyping can help reduce the risk of project failure by identifying potential issues and addressing them early in the process.
- Prototyping can facilitate communication and collaboration among team members and stakeholders, improving overall project efficiency and effectiveness.
- Prototyping can help bridge the gap between technical and non-technical stakeholders by providing a tangible representation of the product.

Disadvantages of the Prototyping Model

- Costly concerning time as well as money.

- There may be too much variation in requirements each time the prototype is evaluated by the customer.
- Poor Documentation due to continuously changing customer requirements.
- It is very difficult for developers to accommodate all the changes demanded by the customer.
- There is uncertainty in determining the number of iterations that would be required before the prototype is finally accepted by the customer.
- After seeing an early prototype, the customers sometimes demand the actual product to be delivered soon.
- Developers in a hurry to build prototypes may end up with sub-optimal solutions.
- The customer might lose interest in the product if he/she is not satisfied with the initial prototype.
- The prototype may not be scalable to meet the future needs of the customer.
- The prototype may not accurately represent the final product due to limited functionality or incomplete features.
- The focus on prototype development may shift away from the final product, leading to delays in the development process.
- The prototype may give a false sense of completion, leading to the premature release of the product.
- The prototype may not consider technical feasibility and scalability issues that can arise during the final product development.
- The prototype may be developed using different tools and technologies, leading to additional training and maintenance costs.
- The prototype may not reflect the actual business requirements of the customer, leading to dissatisfaction with the final product.

Applications of Prototyping Model

- The Prototyping Model should be used when the requirements of the product are not clearly understood or are unstable.
- The prototyping model can also be used if requirements are changing quickly.
- This model can be successfully used for developing user interfaces, high-technology software-intensive systems, and systems with complex algorithms and interfaces.
- The prototyping Model is also a very good choice to demonstrate the technical feasibility of the product.

What is the Hybrid Model?

A hybrid Model is a model which is developed by combining two traditional models of SDLC. The base models can be anyone like a spiral model, V&V model, prototype model, etc. and the selection of models is as per requirements. By collaborating two base models the resulting hybrid Model acquires its properties, process, and benefits which results in building a more powerful, flexible, and effective Model. The combination of traditional models can be like:

- **Spiral and Prototype Model**
- **V&V and Prototype Model**

Why the Hybrid Model?

With the increasing use of agility in software development, the traditional model cannot be sustained as it does not help in fast delivery, achieve a high success rate, and cannot deal with changing customer requirements, this is all due to their lengthy process and standards. So, we need a hybrid Model as it:

- Has the benefits of two individual models.
- Resolve the dependency of models.
- Is suitable for both small and medium-sized systems.
- Involves customers at all phases of development.
- Helps in early delivery.

When To Use a Hybrid Model?

A hybrid Model is developed when we combine two models and this development is useful when:

- The customer is not fixed on its system requirements.
- The requirements of the system cannot be met by using a single SDLC model.
- The organization wants to use agility but complexity is a barrier.
- A fully planned approach to the budget is needed.
- Teams of the organization want collaboration.

It is up to the organization to choose the best possible combination of base models to make a Hybrid Model that can fulfill both business and customer requirements.

Process of Hybrid Model

The hybrid model follows all phases of SDLC along with flexibility in using the required models:

1. **Planning:** The first step to executing any successful work is correct planning and hence the first phase of the Hybrid Model is planning. Planning gives direction and a correct approach to how to do and manage things easily and correctly. In this phase of planning all senior members of an organization like the Product Manager, Delivery Manager, Sales manager, etc. involved and create a plan and explain it to other working members. Planning includes requirement ideas and inputs that help in getting the project execution approach and choosing the correct base models. This phase involves risk analysis, resource planning, and project planning.
2. **Requirements:** In this phase, all requirements needed to develop the system are collected from the client which includes all functional and non-functional requirements of the system. Here, many requirement documents are developed as per the needs of the model. After collecting all requirements the Business Analyst analyzes them and with the help of other senior team members converts them into technical requirements called SRS (System Requirement Specification) which is helpful for the development team.
3. **Design:** In the design phase, the architecture of the system is designed by the team members, they design a working model that specifies how the system will look, how control flows from screen to screen, and shows the functionality of different modules.
4. **Development:** System building starts in this phase by developing the system code. Developers with their team members code the system using any programming language as specified by the organization by maintaining the coding standards. Developers code the

system in module form and after coding the module, they compile it and verify it's working as per requirements.

5. **Integration**: In the integration phase, all tested and verified modules are united to make the complete system as the system is developed by breaking into modules, at a time single module goes through all phases of processing. The integrated product is used as input for testing.
6. **Testing**: Testing means identifying bugs and informing the concerned developer about fixing them. The Testing phase runs parallel to the whole process of the Hybrid model from the start of the Planning phase and ends in the Integration phase. The testing team tests the processing of the system in the form of modules to validate that everything is working as per customer requirements. Testers write test cases and test plans to perform testing.
7. **Deployment**: This is the final stage to hand over the system to the customer. In this phase, the tested developed system is deployed to the customer's deployable environment for its use and experience.
8. **Maintenance**: Taking care of the working system after delivery is called Maintenance. In this phase, after deployment, the customer uses the system and may face real-time issues that the organization needs to fix, and if issues are serious then the system needs to be rolled back to resolve the issue. This phase is also important as it maintains the image of the organization.
9. **Risk Analysis**: This phase defines the risk involved in various phases of the Hybrid Model and it runs parallel to all phases of the Hybrid Model. It identifies the risk areas in different phases and points out them.

Spiral and Prototype Model

This Hybrid Model is a combination of the Spiral Model and Prototype Model.

- **The Spiral Model** is an iterative model combining the features of a linear sequential model in a controlled manner.
- **A prototype Model** is a model in which a brief and simple overview of the system is prepared, tested, reworked, and sent for customer review and verification.

This Hybrid model is used when:

1. There is a dependency.
2. The customer requirements change rapidly with the stages of processing.
3. There is a risk involved in system functioning.
4. Both developers and customers are new to the industry and cannot decide among the available models.

Let's understand the processing of this Hybrid Model with its various stages:

1. Collection of Requirements: Working on software starts with the collection of requirements from the client. All functional and non-functional requirements are gathered from the customer and these requirements are the needs of application development. All senior members of the company are involved in collecting requirements and organizing them in a structured form by documentation which can be BRS and CRS documents. Here in the Hybrid Model, the system is broken down into small modules and developed in modules, not the whole system at a time. The Requirement stage includes further stages like:

- **Prototype Design:** After creating a BRS document from the requirements, a prototype is designed for a particular module which gives a brief overview of the module.
- **Prototype Testing:** After creating the prototype it is sent for testing where the testing team tests it to identify bugs and if the bug is found it is sent for fixing to the respective developer. The tester writes test cases, plans, and test scenarios.
- **Prototype Review:** The tested prototype is forwarded for customer review, where the customer reviews it and gives his opinion on rebuilding and retesting or the prototype is perfect. The above process of prototype goes on until the developing team gets a stable prototype.

2. Design: After getting a stable prototype it is sent for architectural design of the module. The design phase includes the architectural design of the module, workflow, and dependencies among modules.

3. Coding: In the coding phase, the module is coded by developers using their coding language and gives an executable form. The coded module is compiled by developers to confirm its working and dependency with other modules. There is a team of developers working on different modules of the system.

4. Testing: The coded module is finally sent for testing. The testing team tests the module to identify loopholes and if they are successful in catching them then, the module is re-sent to the concerned developer for its fixing, else the module is transferred to the next stage of processing.

After testing, if everything is working as per direction then all modules are developed in the same manner and travel through all the above phases, at last, all modules are united to get a complete compiled system that is deployed to the customer environment for its use.

V&V And Prototype Model

This Hybrid Model is a combination of the V&V Model and Prototype Model.

- **V&V Model:** In this model, V&V stands for Verification and validation, and in this model, both validation and verification of the system go side by side.
- **Prototype Model:** A beautiful model where a prototype is built before developing the actual design of the system. The designed prototype is sent for testing, design, and customer review.

This Hybrid model is used when:

1. The user wants parallel working of the verification and validation process.
2. Good documentation is needed.
3. The customer expects high-quality products with lots of testing.
4. There is no issue of finance and the only requirement is a successful product.

The processing of this Hybrid Model includes the following stages:

1. Requirement Collection: Requirements are the basic needs for the development of software and by only requirement, we can plan its working, decide the processing needs, coding language, team members, number of days to deliver, and much more. The requirements of the system are collected from customers which go for documentation and testing. The requirements collected from the customer are further converted into a CRS document that contains simple, non-technical requirements and is sent to the tester where:

- Tester reviewed the CRS document.
- Write Acceptance Testing by preparing test cases and test plans.

2. BRS and Prototype Design: The CRS document developed in the previous stage is used to build a BRS document by Business Analyst which contains technical information for its understanding at the business level. BRS contains bar graphs, data flow diagrams, ER diagrams, etc. From the BRS web developers design and develop a prototype which is reviewed and sent for testing. in testing testers:

- Review the document.
- Carry out System testing.

After that, testers test the prototype if some bug is found it is sent for fixing to the design team. The tested prototype is sent for customer review and verification. In case the customer is not satisfied with the designed prototype it is sent for rebuilding it is forwarded to the next processing stage.

3. HLD (High-Level design): After getting a customer-approved prototype it is sent to HLD, where its architecture is designed and understood by developers. Different technical approaches are involved to design the best feasible architecture which includes workflow, dependencies, functionalities of modules, database design, tables, and interface relationships. The designed HLD is passed to the next stage of testing, where testers:

- Review the HLD.
- Write Integration Testing documents and write test cases and test plans to execute the testing process.

4. LLD (Low-Level Design): This phase is for designing the LLD document of the prototype. In this phase, the LLD document is prepared which contains detailed information about the working prototype like the type of programming language, compatibility of all modules, and functioning of modules. After designing the LLD it is sent for testing, where the tester:

- Review the LLD.
- Write functional Testing, test cases, and test plans to carry out the testing process.

5. Coding: This phase includes coding of the particular prototypes by the developers using their coding language as directed by their team leaders, the coding must follow all coding standards and guidelines. The coded prototype goes for testing, where testers perform Unit Box testing to find bugs and check extreme conditions of the module.

This process is going on until we get stable prototypes and all modules. And at last, it is delivered to the customer.

Advantages of Hybrid Model

- **The benefit of two models:** By using the Hybrid Model users can take advantage of two models, one shade the negativity of another.
- **Fixed Pattern:** A defined pattern of base models is to be followed to carry out the whole processing by which no need to decide on new planning and architecture of the model.

- **High Output**: The success rate of the model increases with less rejection of the system at the delivery time which finally increases the value of the developer team.
- **Satisfaction**: Customers satisfaction with the effective working system as they receive a successful system in less delivery time.

Disadvantages of the Hybrid Model

- **Complexity:** Not successful in the case of large and complex systems and is only effective for small and medium-sized systems. With a large system, the complexity increases in handling two models together.
- **Not economic:** The cost of the system increases many folds as lots of changes occur and sometimes many steps are to be re-work.
- **Uneven working**: The working of all hybrid models is not the same the same pattern for all hybrid models can't be followed.

Software Testing Life cycle:

It is Step by Step Procedure to test a software. It contains multiple stages like

- System study
- Prepare Test plan
- Write Test Cases
- Traceability Matrix
- Test Execution
- Defect Tracking
- Prepare a Test execution report and send it to the customer.
- Retrospect meeting
- **System Study**

This is the stage where we discuss here how we understood the complete requirement and if you have any queries this is the stage where we get clarity.

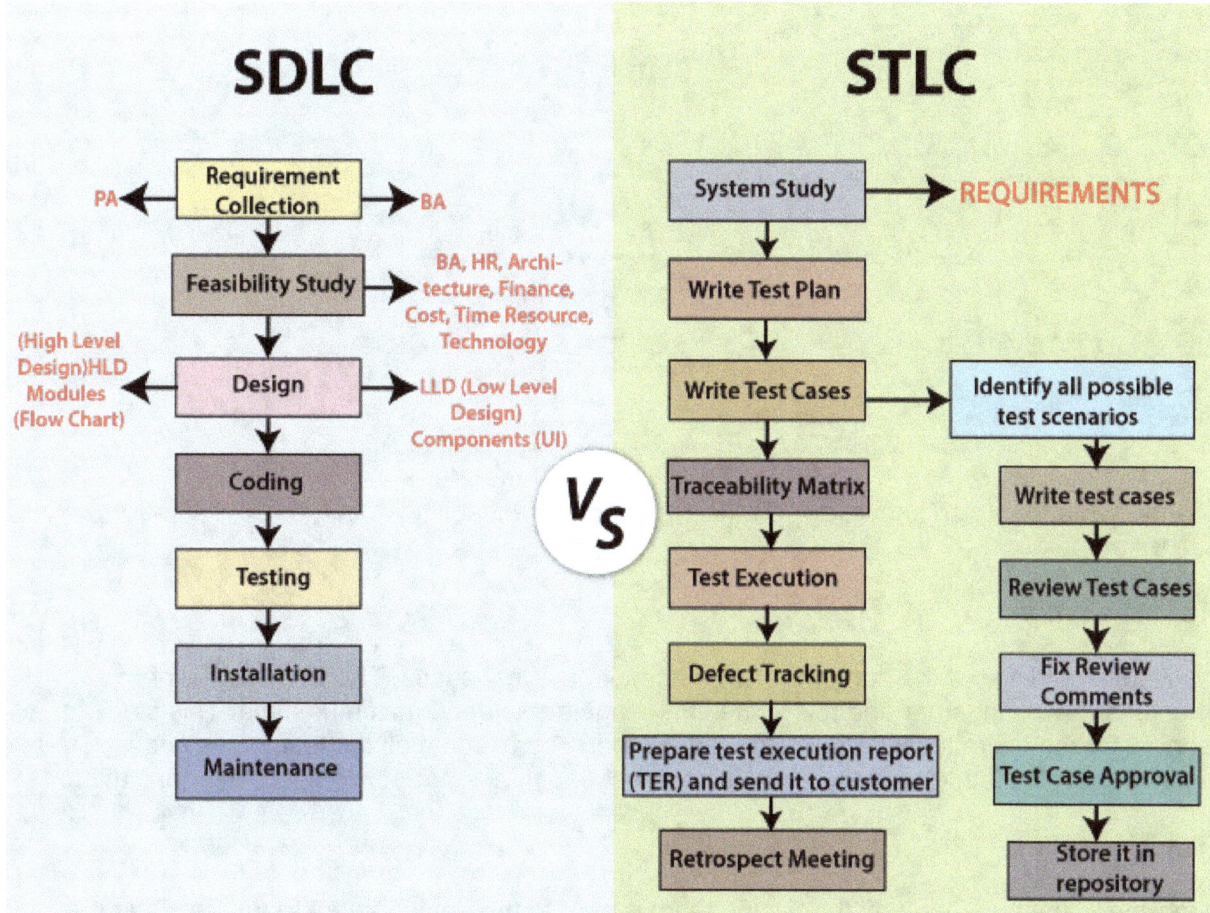

- **Test Plan**

Test Plan is a document which derives all future activities of the project. All future testing activities are planned and put into a document and this document is known as Test Plan. It contains – number of engineers needed for the project, who should test which feature, how the defects must be communicated to the development team, when we should start and finish writing test cases, executing test cases, what are the types of testing we use to test for the application etc.

- **Write Test Case**

Test case is a document which contains all possible scenarios. Write test case – we write test cases for each feature. These test cases are reviewed, and after all mistakes are corrected and once the test cases are approved – then they are stored in the test case repository.

- **Traceability Matrix**

Traceability Matrix – it is a document which ensures that every requirement has a test case.

Test cases are written by looking at the requirements and test cases are executed by looking at the test cases. If any requirement is missed i.e, test cases are not written for a particular requirement, then that particular feature is not tested which may have some bugs. Just to ensure that all the requirements are converted, traceability matrix is written. This is shown below

Requirements Traceability Matrix

Project Name:	TestKarts.com													
Project Manager:	Manager Testkarts.com													
Project Description:	Testing and Development project for the fresher and experience learner.													

Requirements					Testing								
Req. ID	Requirements Description	Requirements Source	Requirement Type	WBS Deliverables	Test Case ID	Test Description	TEST	UAT	QA	PROD	PRE-PROD	NON-PROD	Defective	Defe
REQ001	User registration functionality	Business Analyst	Functional	WBS-001	TC001	Verify user can successfully register an account	Pass	Pass	Pass	Pass	Fail		No	
REQ001	User registration functionality	Business Analyst	Functional	WBS-001	TC002	Verify error message is displayed for invalid inputs	N/A	Fail	Pass	Fail	N/A		Yes	DEF00
REQ001	User registration functionality	Business Analyst	Functional	WBS-001	TC003	Verify user receives a confirmation email	Pass	N/A	Fail	N/A	Pass		Yes	DEF00
REQ002	Login functionality	Product Owner	Functional	WBS-002	TC004	Verify user can log in with valid credentials	Fail	Pass	N/A	N/A	N/A		NO	
REQ002	Login functionality	Product Owner	Functional	WBS-002	TC005	Verify error message is displayed for incorrect login	Fail	Fail	N/A	Pass	Fail		Yes	DEF00
REQ002	Login functionality	Product Owner	Functional	WBS-002	TC006	Verify "Forgot Password" link redirects correctly	Fail	Fail	N/A	Pass	Pass		No	
REQ003	Create new post	User Stories	Functional	WBS-003	TC007	Verify user can create a new post				N/A	N/A		No	
REQ003	Create new post	User Stories	Functional	WBS-003	TC008	Verify error message is displayed for empty content	Pass	Pass	Pass	Fail	Fail		Yes	DEF00

The Traceability Matrix is also known as RTM(Requirement Traceability Matrix) or CRM(Cross Reference Matrix).

- **Test Execution:**

Test execution is nothing but the stage where we execute the test cases. This is a stage where all the engineer's are work together and this is the time engineers spend maximum time. This stage is very important for the entire testing, this is the stage where we execute all the test cases and identify maximum defect and this is the stage where test engineer's are efficient to the organization.

Defect Tracking

Defect Tracking – any bug found by the testing team is sent to the development team. This bug has to be checked by the testing team if it has been fixed by the developers.

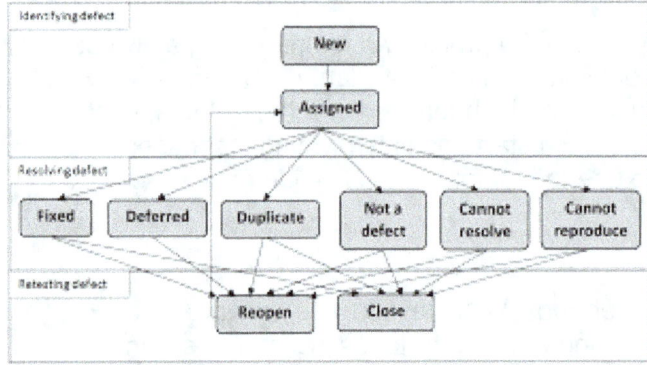

- **Test Execution Report:**

Test Execution Report :- Send it to customer – contains a list of bugs(major, minor and critical), summary of test pass, fail etc and when this is sent, according to the customer – the project is over.

TER is prepared after every test cycle and sent to the development team, testing team, management and customer(depending if it is a fixed bid project or time & material bid project).

The last TER of the last test cycle is always sent to the customer. And this means that the project is over-according to the customer.

- **Retrospect meeting:**

Retrospect meeting – (also called Post Mortem Meeting / Project Closure Meeting)

The Test Manager calls everyone in the testing team for a meeting and asks them for a list of mistakes and achievements in the project.

MISTAKES(Mistakes in the Process)

ACHIEVEMENTS(good process/procedure followed)

1) Review process is not good

1)Last day of each cycle generally swap modules and do ad-hoc testing

….

…..

…..

…..

…..

….

This is done by the test lead or test manager. Here, the manager documents this retrospect meeting and stores it in QMS (Quality Management System). It is a folder, where inside this folder, there is another folder called Retrospect folder and here this excel sheet document is stored. When we get a new project, while we write the test plan – we will open this retrospect file and will try and implement the good practices and correct the mistakes.

When you join a company, always ask for –
- Requirements of the project
- Test plan of the project
- Test cases(existing) of the project
- Application which is to be developed

Test Plan:

Test plan is a document which drives all future testing activities.

Test plan is prepared by Test manager(20%), Test Engineer(20%) and by Test Lead(60%).

There are 15 sections in a test plan. We will look at each one of them below

1. Objective:

It gives the aim of preparing a test plan i.e, why are we preparing this test plan.

2. Effort Estimation

- This section covers estimation of How long it would take to complete the testing.
- How many engineers are needed to complete the testing.
- What is the cost required to complete the entire testing?

3. Scope

Scope: It contains information that needs to be tested with respect to an application. The Scope can be further divided into two parts:

- In scope
- Out scope

In scope: These are the modules that need to be tested rigorously (in-detail).

Out scope: These are the modules, which need not be tested rigorously.

For example, Suppose we have a Gmail application to test, where **features to be tested** such as **Compose mail, Sent Items, Inbox, Drafts** and the **features which not be tested** such as **Help**, and so on which means that in the planning stage, we will decide that which functionality has to be checked or not based on the time limit given in the product.

Now **how do we decide which features not to be tested?**

We have the following aspects where we can decide which feature not to be tested:

- As we see above, that **Help** feature is not going to be tested, as it is written and developed by the technical writer and reviewed by another professional writer.
- Let us assume that we have one application that has **P, Q, R, and S** features, which need to be developed based on the requirements. But here, the S feature has already been designed and used by some other company. So the development team will purchase S from that company and integrate with additional features such as P, Q, and R.

Now, we will not perform functional testing on the S feature because it has already been used in real-time. But we will do the integration testing, and system testing between P, Q, R, and S features because the new features might not work correctly with S feature as we can see in the below image:

- Suppose in the first release of the product, the elements that have been developed, such as **P, Q, R, S, T, U, V, W.....X, Y, Z**. Now the client will provide the requirements for the new features which improve the product in the second release and the new features are **A1, B2, C3, D4, and E5**.

After that, we will write the scope during the test plan as

Scope

Features to be tested

A1, B2, C3, D4, E5 (new features)

P, Q, R, S, T

Features not to be tested

W…..X, Y, Z

Therefore, we will check the new features first and then continue with the old features because that might be affected after adding the new features, which means it will also affect the impact areas, so we will do one round of regressing testing for P, Q, R…, T features.

4. Approach

The way we go about testing the product in future,

a) By writing high level scenarios

b) By writing flow graphs

- **By writing the high-level scenarios**

For example, suppose we are testing the **Gmail** application:

- Login to Gmail- sends an email and check whether it is in the Sent Items page
- Login to …….
- ……
- ……..

We are writing this to describe the approaches which have to be taken for testing the product and only for the critical features where we will write the high-level scenarios. Here, we will not be focusing on covering all the scenarios because it can be decided by the particular test engineer that which features have to be tested or not.

By Writing flow Graphs:

The flow graph is written because writing the high-level scenarios are bit time taking process, as we can see in the below image:

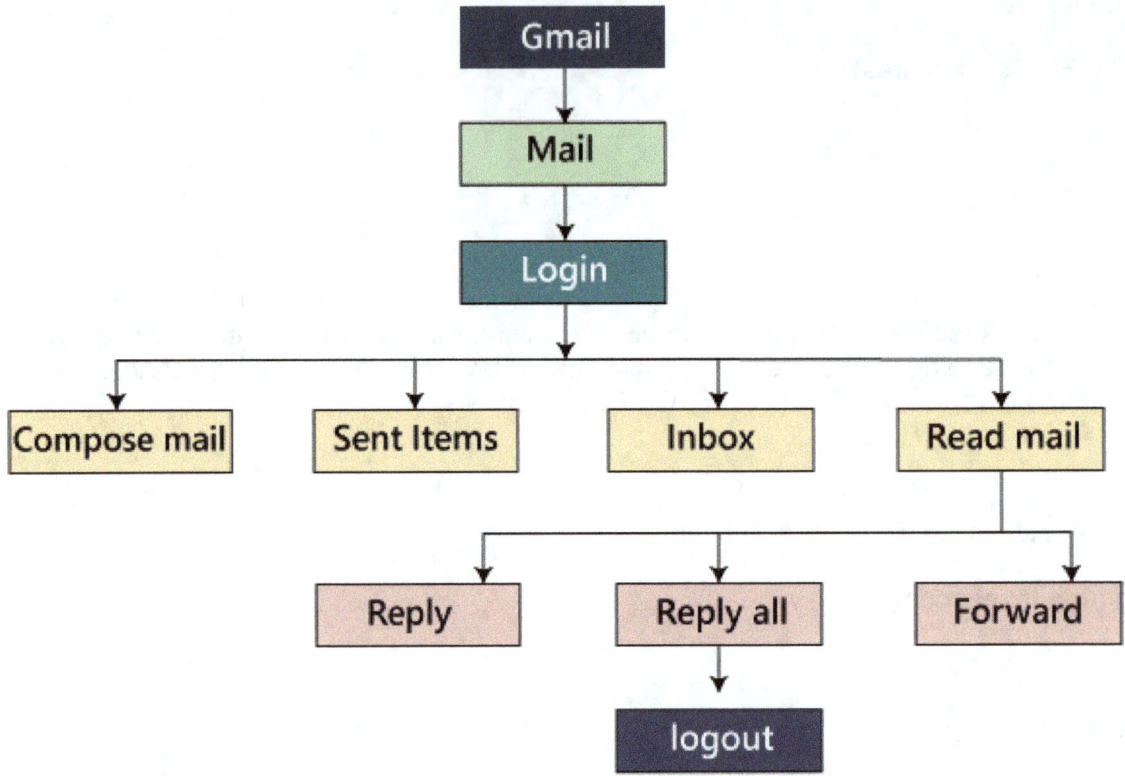

We are creating flow graphs to make the following benefits such as:

- Coverage is easy
- Merging is easy

The approach can be classified into two parts which are as following:

- Top to bottom approach
- Bottom to top approach

5. Assumptions:

It contains information about a problem or issue which may have occurred during the testing process and when we are writing the test plans, the assured assumptions would be made like resources and technologies, etc.

6. Risk

These are the challenges which we need to face to test the application in the current release and if the assumptions will fail then the risks are involved.

For example, the effect for an application release date becomes postponed.

7. Mitigation plan or contingency plan

It is a back-up plan which is prepared to overcome the risks or issues.

Let us see one example for assumption, risk, and the contingency plan together because they are co-related to each other.

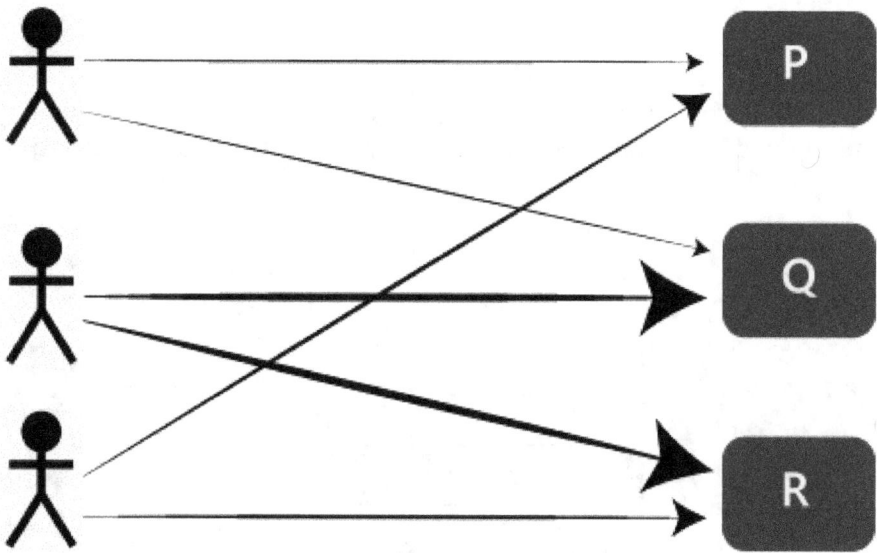

In any product, the **assumption** we will make is that the all 3 test engineers will be there until the completion of the product and each of them is assigned different modules such as P, Q, and R. In this particular scenario, the **risk** could be that if the test engineer left the project in the middle of it.

Therefore, the **contingency plan** will be assigned a primary and subordinate owner to each feature. So if the one test engineer leaves, the subordinate owner takes over that specific feature and also helps the new test engineer, so he/she can understand their assigned modules.

The assumptions, risk, and mitigation or contingency plan are always precise on the product itself. The various types of risks are as follows:

- Customer perspective
- Resource approach
- Technical opinion

8. Test methodology:

It contains information about performing a different kind of testing like Functional testing, Integration testing, and System testing, etc. on the application. In this, we will decide what type of testing; we will perform on the various features based on the application requirement. And here, we should also define what kind of testing we will use in the testing methodologies so that everyone, like the management, the development team, and the testing team can understand easily because the testing terms are not standard.

For example, for standalone application such as **Adobe Photoshop**, we will perform the following types of testing:

Smoke testing→ Functional testing → Integration testing →System testing →Adhoc testing → Compatibility testing → Regression testing→ Globalization testing → Accessibility testing → Usability testing → Reliability testing → Recovery testing → Installation or Uninstallation testing

9. Test Schedule:

It is used to explain the timing to work, which needs to be done or this attribute covers when exactly each testing activity should start and end? And the exact data is also mentioned for every testing activity for the particular date.

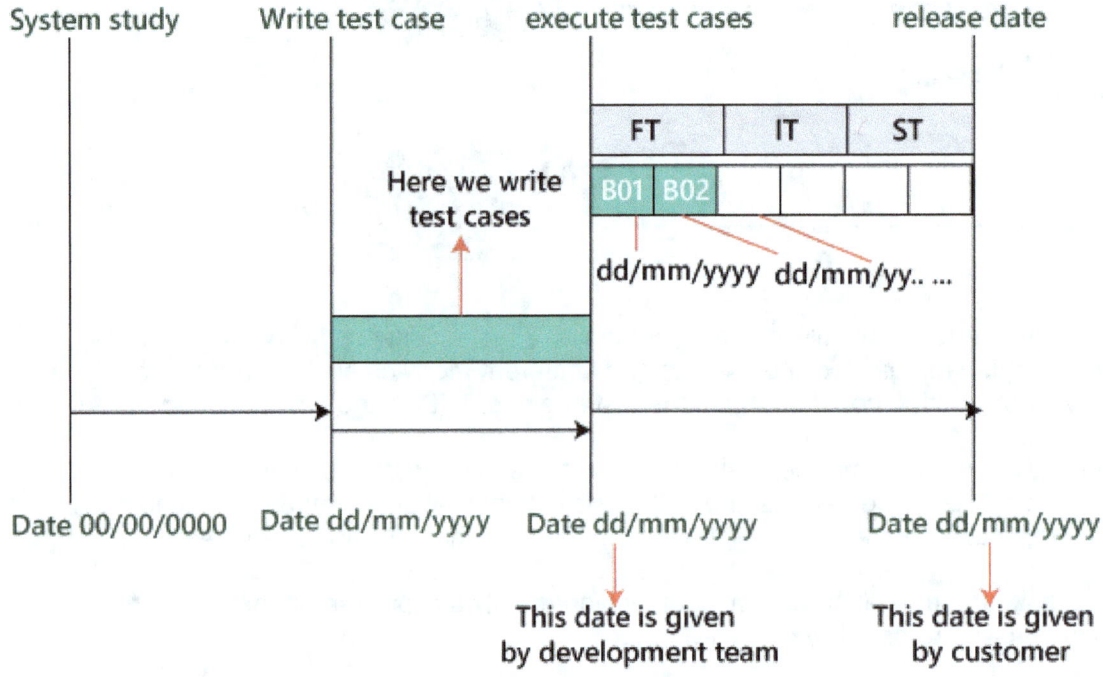

Therefore as we can see in the above image that for the particular activity, there will be a starting date and ending date; for each testing to a specific build, there will be the specified date.

For example
- Writing test cases
- Execution process

10. Test Environment

These are the environments where we will test the application, and here we have two types of environments, which are software and **hardware** configuration.

The **software configuration** means the details about different **Operating Systems** such as **Windows, Linux, UNIX, and Mac** and various **Browsers** like **Google Chrome, Firefox, Opera, Internet Explorer**, and so on.

And the **hardware configuration** means the information about different sizes of **RAM, ROM, and the Processors**.

For example

- The **Software** includes the following:

Server:

Operating system - Linux

Web Server- Apache Tomcat

Application server-Web sphere

Database server -Oracle - MS-SQL server

Note: The above servers are the servers that are used by the testing team to test the application.

Client:

Operating System-Window XP, Vista 7

Browsers-Mozilla Firefox, Google Chrome, Internet Explorer, Internet Explorer 7, and Internet Explorer 8

Note: The above details provide the various operating systems and browsers in which the testing team will test the application.

- The **Hardware** includes the following:

Server: Sun StarCat 1500

This particular server can be used by the testing team to test their application.

Client:

It has the following configuration, which is as follows:

Processor-Intal2GHz

RAM-2GB

Note:Note: It will provide the configuration of the systems of the test engineers that is the testing team.

- **Process to install the software**
  ……

.....
.....

The development team will provide the configuration of how to install the software. If the development team will not yet provide the process, then we will write it as Task-Based Development (TBD) in the test plan.

11. Test Automation:

In this, we will decide the following:

- Which feature has to be automated and not to be automated?
- Which test automation tool we are going to use on which automation framework?

We automate the test case only after the first release.

Here the question arises that on what basis **we** will **decide which features have to be tested?**

In the above image, we can see that the most commonly used features need to be tested again and again. Suppose we have to check the Gmail application where the essential features are **Compose mail, Sent Items, and Inbox**. So we will test these features because while performing manual testing, it takes more time, and it also becomes a monotonous job.

Now, **how do we decide which features are not going to be tested?**

Suppose **the Help** feature of the Gmail application is not tested again and again because these features are not regularly used, so we do not need to check it frequently.

But **if some features are unstable and have lots of bugs**, which means that we will not test those features because it has to be tested again and again while doing manual testing.

If **there is a feature that has to be tested frequently**, we are expecting the requirement change for that feature, so we do not check it because changing the manual test cases is more comfortable as compared to change in the automation test script.

12. Defect Tracking

In this section, we mention – how to communicate the defects found during testing to the development team and also how the development team should respond to it. We should also mention the priority of the defect – high, medium, low.

12.1 Procedure to track the defect

....

....

....

....

12.2 Defect tracking tool

We mention the name of the tool we will be using to track the defects

12.3 Severity

12.3.1 Blocker(or Showstopper)

….

…. (define it with an example in the test plan)

For ex, there will be bug in the module. We cannot go and test the other modules because this blocker has blocked the other modules.

12.3.2 Critical

…

… (define it with an example)

Bugs which affects the business is considered critical

12.3.3 Major

…

… (define it with an example)

Bugs which affects look and feel of the application is considered as major

12.3.4 Minor

…

… (define it with an example)

12.4 Priority

12.4.1 High – P1

…

12.4.2 Medium – P2

…

12.4.3 Low – P3

…

…

... P4

So, depending on the priority of the defect (high, medium or low), we classify it as P1, P2, P3, P4.

13. Test Deliverable

These are the documents which are the output from the testing team, which we handed over to the customer along with the product. It includes the following:

- **Test plan**
- **Test Cases**
- **Test Scripts**
- **RTM(Requirement Traceability Matrix)**
- **Defect Report**
- **Test Execution Report**
- **Graphs and metrics**
- **Release Notes**

Graph and Matrices

Graph

In this, we will discuss the types of **graphs** we will send, and we will also provide a sample of each graph.

As we can see, we have five different graphs that show the various aspects of the testing process.

Graph1: In this, we will show how many defects have been identified and how many defects have been fixed in every module.

Graph 2: Figure one shows how many critical, major, and minor defects have been identified for every module and how many have been fixed for their respective modules.

Graph3: In this particular graph, we represent the **build wise graph**, which means that in every build how many defects have been identified and fixed for every module. Based on the module, we have determined the bugs. We will add **R** to show the number of defects in P and Q, and we also add **S** to show the defects in P, Q, and R.

Graph4: The test lead will design the **Bug Trend analysis** graph which is created every month and send it to the Management as well. And it is just like a prediction which is done at the end of the product. And here, we can also **rate the bug fixes** as we can observe that **arc** has an **upward tendency** in the below image.

Graph5: The **Test Manager** has designed this type of graph. This graph is intended to understand the gap in the assessment of bugs and the actual bugs which have occurred, and this graph also helps to improve the evaluation of bugs in the future.

Metrics

As above, we create the bug distribution graph, which is in the figure 1, and with the help of above mentioned data, we will design the metrics as well.

For example

In the above figure, we retain the records of all the test engineers in a particular project and how many defects have been identified and fixed. We can also use this data for future analysis. When a new requirement comes, we can decide whom to provide the challenging feature for testing based on the number of defects they have found earlier according to the above metrics. And we will be in a better situation to know who can handle the problematic features very well and find maximum numbers of defects.

Release Note: It is a document that is prepared during the release of the product and signed by the Test Manager.

In the below image, we can see that the final product is developed and deployed to the customer, and the latest release name is **Beta**.

The **Release note** consists of the following:

- User manual.
- List of pending and open defects.
- List of added, modified, and deleted features.
- List of the platform (Operating System, Hardware, Browsers) on which the product is tested.
- Platform in which the product is not tested.
- List of bugs fixed in the current release, and the list of fixed bugs in the previous release.
- Installation process
- Versions of the software

For Example

Suppose that **Beta** is the second release of the application after the first release **Alpha** is released. Some of the defects identified in the first release and that has been fixed in the later release. And here, we will also point out the list of newly added, modified, and deleted features from alpha release to the beta release.

14.Test stop criteria:

This Section covers when we do stop Testing

1.We stop testing in two different cases

- If the software quality is good means and if the software quality is bad means.
- Software quality good means all the feature requested by the customer should be ready
- All the end to end business scenarios should work fine.
- There should be zero blocker and zero critical defect
- If there are few bugs left out it should be written within the limit set by the customer
- you should have tested the software in an environment similar to the production environment.

Software quality bad means

- If there are too many blocker and Critical defect
- If many end to end business scenarios are not working fine.

- If it is crossing the budget and also the schedule.

15. Entry and Exit Criteria:

Before we start with Functional Testing, all the above entry criteria should be met.

After we are done with FT, before we start with Integration Testing, then the exit criteria of FT should be met. The percentage of exit criteria is decided by meeting with both the development and test manager. They compromise and conclude the percentage. If the exit criteria of FT is not met, then we cannot move onto IT.

Based on severity of defects means,

The testing team would have decided that in order to move onto the next stage, the following criteria should be met,

- There should not be more than 20 critical bugs
- There should not be more than 60 major bugs
- There should not be more than 100 minor bugs.

If all the above are met, then they move onto the next testing stage.

But the problem with the above method was,

21 critical, 50 major, 99 minor – cant exit because there are more than 20 critical bugs.

10 critical, 90 major, 200 minor – can exit. But the 10 critical bugs can affect the product.

Thus, they came up with the concept of "weight of defects''. i.e, 3 major = 1 critical, 5 minor – 1 critical and total critical should not be more than 60.

So, for,

21 critical – 21

50 major – 16 critical

99 minor – 19 critical

Totally there are 56 critical bugs, so we can move onto the next stage.

But for the 2nd example, we cannot move on.

Entry criteria for IT :

- should have met exit criteria of FT

…

…

...

(remaining all are same as entry criteria of FT)

Exit criteria for IT :

...

...

...

All points are the same as exit criteria for FT.

But if the %age pass for FT is 85%, then the %age pass for IT should be 90% - because as we reach the later stages of testing, we expect the number of defects to be less.

Entry criteria for ST :

- exit criteria of IT should be met

- minimum set of features must be developed

- test environment should be similar to production environment

...

...

(remaining all are same as of IT)

Exit criteria for ST :

- everything remains the same as above, but the pass %age is now 99% - there should be 0 critical bugs. There could be some 30 major and 50 minor bugs. If all this is met, then the product can be released.

Note : All the numbers given above are just for example sake. They are not international standard numbers!!!.

Here **based on the severity** of the bug's means that the testing team would have decided to proceed further for the next phases.

16. Role & Responsibility

It defines the complete task which needs to be performed by the entire testing team. When a large project comes, then the **Test Manager** is a person who writes the test plan. If there are 3-4 small projects, then the test manager will assign each project to each Test Lead. And then, the test lead writes the test plan for the project, which he/she is assigned.

Let see one example where we will understand the roles and responsibility of the Test manager, test lead, and the test engineers.

Role: Test Manager

Name: Ryan

Responsibility:

- Prepare(write and review) the test plan
- Conduct the meeting with the development team
- Conduct the meeting with the testing team
- Conduct the meeting with the customer
- Conduct one monthly stand up meeting
- Sign off release note
- Handling Escalations and issues

Role: Test Lead

Name: Harvey

Responsibility:

- Prepare(write and review) the test plan
- Conduct daily stand up meeting
- Review and approve the test case
- Prepare the RTM and Reports
- Assign modules
- Handling schedule

Role: Test Engineer 1, Test Engineer 2 and Test Engineer 3

Name: Louis, Jessica, Donna

Assign modules: M1, M2, and M3

Responsibility:

- Write, Review, and Execute the test documents which consists of test case and test scenarios
- Read, review, understand and analysis the requirement
- Write the flow of the application
- Execute the test case
- RTM for respective modules
- Defect tracking
- Prepare the test execution report and communicate it to the Test Lead.

17. Template

This part contains all the templates for the documents that will be used in the product, and all the test engineers will use only these templates in the project to maintain the consistency of the product. Here, we have different types of the template which are used during the entire testing process such as:

- Test case template
- Test case review template
- RTM Template
- Bug Report Template
- Test execution Report

Let us see one sample of test plan document

Page-1

Page3-page18

Page-20

In-Page 1, we primarily fill only the **Versions, Author, Comments, and Reviewed By** fields, and after the manager approves it, we will mention the details in the **Approved By and Approval Date** fields.

Mostly the test plan is approved by the Test Manager, and the test engineers only review it. And when the new features come, we will modify the test plan and do the necessary modification in the Version field, and then it will be sent again for further review, update, and approval of the manager. The test plan must be updated whenever any changes have occurred. On page 20, the **References** specify the details about all the documents which we are going to use to write the test plan document.

Note:

Who writes the test plan?

- Test Lead→60%
- Test Manager→20%
- Test Engineer→20%

Therefore, as we can see from above that in 60% of the product, the test plan is written by the Test Lead.

Who reviews the Test Plan?

- Test Lead
- Test Manager
- Test engineer
- Customer
- Development team

The Test Engineer reviews the Test plan for their module perspective and the test manager reviews the Test plan based on the customer opinion.

Who approves the test Plan?

- Customer

- Test Manager

Who writes the test case?

- Test Lead
- Test Engineer

Who reviewed the test case?

- Test Engineer
- Test Lead
- Customer
- Development Team

Who approves the Test cases?

- Test Manager
- Test Lead
- Customer

Requirement Traceability Matrix:

We have learnt about TM earlier. Once the missing requirements are identified – we write the test cases for the requirements which we have missed – review it and get it approved – and then store the test cases in the repository and then fill in the name of the test case for which the requirements have been missed.

Traceability Matrix is a document which has got the mapping between requirements and test cases. We write TM to make sure that every requirement has at least 1 test case.

This document is designed to make sure that each requirement has a test case, and the test case is written based on business needs, which are given by the client. It will be performed with the help of the test cases if any requirement is missing, which means that the test case is not written for a particular need, and that specific requirement is not tested because it may have some bugs. The traceability is written to make sure that the entire requirement is covered.

.

We can observe in the below image that the requirement number 2 and 4 test case names are not mentioned that's why we highlighted them, so that we can easily understand that we have to write the test case for them

Generally, this is like a worksheet document, which contains a table, but there are also many user-defined templates for the traceability matrix. Each requirement in the traceability matrix is connected with its respective test case so that tests can be carried out sequentially according to specific requirements.

Note:

We go for RTM after approval and before execution so that we don't miss out on any Test Case for any requirement.

We don't write RTM while writing the testing because it can be incomplete, and after writing the test case, we don't go here because the test case can be rejected.

The RTM document ensures that at least there is one test case written in each requirement, whereas it does not talk about all possible test cases written for the particular requirement.

RTM Template

Below is the sample template of requirement traceability matrix (RTM):

Example of RTM template

Let us one sample of RTM template for better understanding:

Goals of Traceability Matrix

- It helps in tracing the documents that are developed during various phases of SDLC.
- It ensures that the software completely meets the customer's requirements.
- It helps in detecting the root cause of any bug.

Types of Traceability Test Matrix

The traceability matrix can be classified into three different types which are as follows:

- Forward traceability
- Backward or reverse traceability
- Bi-directional traceability

Forward traceability

The forward traceability test matrix is used to ensure that every business's needs or requirements are executed correctly in the application and also tested rigorously. The main objective of this is to verify whether the product developments are going in the right direction. In this, the requirements are mapped into the forward direction to the test cases.

Backward or reverse traceability

The reverse or backward traceability is used to check that we are not increasing the space of the product by enhancing the design elements, code, and testing other things which are not mentioned in the business needs. And the main objective of this is that the existing project remains in the correct direction. In this, the requirements are mapped into the backward direction to the test cases.

Bi-directional traceability

It is a combination of forwarding and backward traceability matrix, which is used to make sure that all the business needs are executed in the test cases. It also evaluates the modification in the requirement which is occurring due to the bugs in the application.

Advantage of RTM

Following are the benefits of requirement traceability matrix:

- With the help of the RTM document, we can display the complete test execution and bugs status based on requirements.
- It is used to show the missing requirements or conflicts in documents.
- In this, we can ensure complete test coverage, which means all the modules are tested.
- It will also consider the efforts of the testing teamwork towards reworking or reconsidering the test cases.

The testing quality depends on,

- Mood of the TE
- Testing is not consistent
- Varies from person to person

So, we write test cases.

Test case is a document which covers all possible scenarios to test all the feature(s).

It is a set of input parameters for which the software will be tested. The SRS are numbered so that developers and testing team will not miss out on any feature.

When do we write test cases?

Customer gives requirements – developer start developing and they say they need about 4 months to develop this product – during this time, testing team start writing test cases – once it is done, they send it to test lead who reviews it and adds some more scenarios – developers finish developing the product and the product is given for testing – the test engineer then looks at the test cases and starts testing the product – the TE never looks at the requirements while testing the product – thus testing is consistent and does not depend on the mood and quality of the test engineer.

The list of values derived to test the Amount text field is – Blank, -100, hundred, 100, 6000, Rs100, $100, $+?, 0100, Blank Space 100, 100.50, 0, 90

When writing test cases, actual results should never be written as the product is still being developed. Only after execution of test cases should the actual result be written.

Why do we write test cases?

- To have better test coverage – cover all possible scenarios and document it, so that we need not remember all the scenarios
- To have consistency in test case execution – seeing the test case and testing the product
- To avoid training every new engineer on the product – when an engineer leaves, he leaves with a lot of knowledge and scenarios. Those scenarios should be documented, so that new engineers can test with the given scenarios and also write new scenarios.
- To depend on process rather than on a person

Let's say a test engineer has tested a product during 1st release, 2nd release and has left the company for the 3rd release. As this TE has mastered a module and has tested the application rigorously by deriving many values. If that person is not there for 3rd release, it becomes difficult for the new person – hence all the derived values are documented, so that it can be used in feature.

When developers are developing the 1st product (1st release), TE writes test cases. In the 2nd release, when new features are added, TE writes test cases. In the next release, when features are modified – TE modifies test cases or writes new test cases.

Test case template

The primary purpose of writing a test case is to achieve the efficiency of the application.

As we know, the **actual result** is written after the test case execution, and most of the time, it would be the same as the **expected result**. But if the test step fails, it will be different. So, the actual result field can be skipped, and in **the Comments** section, we can write about the bugs.

And also, the **Input field** can be removed, and this information can be added to the **Description field**.

The template we discuss above is not the standard one because it can be different for each company and also with each application, which is based on the test engineer and the test lead. But, for testing one application, all the test engineers should follow a usual template, which is formulated.

The test case should be written in simple language so that a new test engineer can also understand and execute the same.

In the above sample template, the header contains the following:

Step number

It is also essential because if step number 20 is failing, we can document the bug report and hence prioritize working and also decide if it's a critical bug.

Test case type

It can be functional, integration or system test cases or positive or negative or positive and negative test cases.

Release

One release can contain many versions of the release.

Pre-condition

These are the necessary conditions that need to be satisfied by every test engineer before starting the test execution process. Or it is the data configuration or the data setup that needs to be created for the testing.

For example: In an application, we are writing test cases to add users, edit users, and delete users. The per-condition will be seen if user A is added before editing it and removing it.

Test data

These are the values or the input we need to create as per the per-condition.

For example, Username, Password, and account number of the users.

The test lead may be given the test data like username or password to test the application, or the test engineer may themself generate the username and password.

Severity

The severity can be **major, minor, and critical**, the severity in the test case talks about the importance of that particular test case. All the text execution process always depends on the severity of the test cases.

We can choose the severity based on the module. There are many features included in a module, even if one element is critical, we claim that test case to be critical. It depends on the functions for which we are writing the test case.

For example, we will take the Gmail application and let us see the severity based on the modules:

Modules	Severity
Login	Critical
Help	Minor
Compose mail	Critical
Setting	Minor
Inbox	Critical
Sent items	Major
Logout	Critical

And for the banking application, the severity could be as follows:

Modules	Severity
Amount transfer	critical
Feedback	minor

Brief description

The test engineer has written a test case for a particular feature. If he/she comes and reads the test cases for the moment, he/she will not know for what feature has written it. So, the brief description will help them in which feature test cases are written.

Example of a test case template

Here, we are writing a test case for the **ICICI application's Login** module:

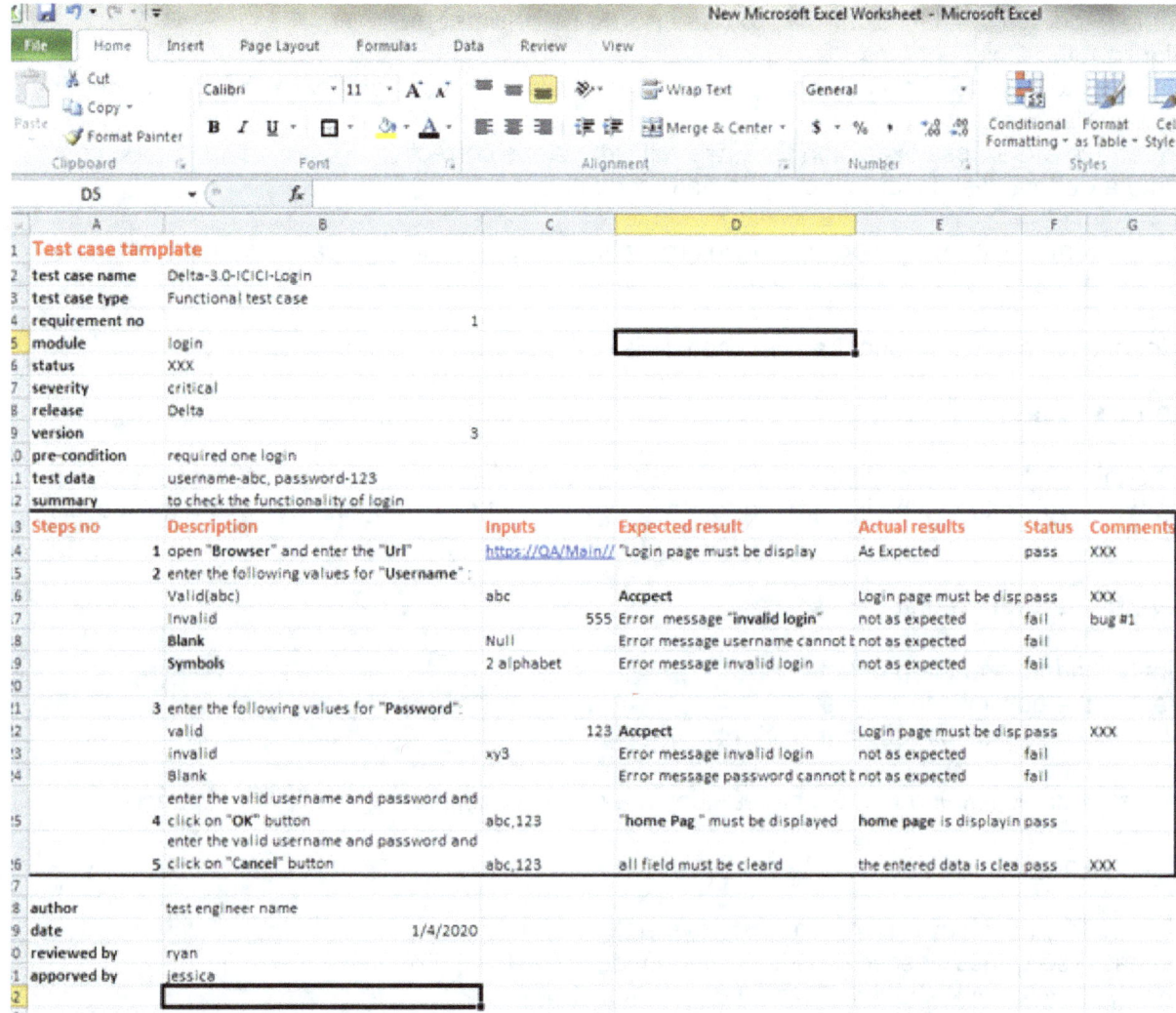

Types of test cases

We have a different kind of test cases, which are as follows:

- **Function test cases**
- **Integration test cases**
- **System test cases**

The functional test cases

Firstly, we check for which field we will write test cases and then describe accordingly.

In functional testing or if the application is data-driven, we require the input column else; it is a bit time-consuming.

Rules to write functional test cases:

- In the expected results column, try to use **should be** or **must be**.
- Highlight the Object names.
- We have to describe only those steps which we require the most; otherwise, we do not need to define all the steps.
- To reduce the excess execution time, we will write steps correctly.
- Write a generic test case; do not try to hard code it.

Let say it is the amount transfer module, so we are writing the functional test cases for it and then also specify that it is not a login feature.

The functional test case for amount transfer module is in the below Excel file:

Integration test case

In this, we should not write something which we already covered in the functional test cases, and something we have written in the integration test case should not be written in the system test case again.

Rules to write integration test cases

- Firstly, understand the product
- Identify the possible scenarios
- Write the test case based on the priority

When the test engineer writing the test cases, they may need to consider the following aspects:

If the test cases are in details:

- They will try to achieve maximum test coverage.
- All test case values or scenarios are correctly described.
- They will try to think about the execution point of view.
- The template which is used to write the test case must be unique.

Note: when we involve fewer numbers of steps or coverage is more, it should be the best test case, and when these test cases are given to anyone, they will understand easily.

System test cases

We will write the system test cases for the end-to-end business flows. And we have the entire modules ready to write the system test cases.

The process to write test cases

The method of writing a test case can be completed into the following steps, which are as below:

System study

In this, we will understand the application by looking at the requirements or the SRS, which is given by the customer.

Identify all scenarios:

- When the product is launched, what are the possible ways the end-user may use the software to identify all the possible ways.
- I have documented all possible scenarios in a document, which is called test design/high-level design.
- The test design is a record having all the possible scenarios.

Write test cases

Convert all the identified scenarios to test claims and group the scenarios related to their features, prioritize the module, and write test cases by applying test case design techniques and use the standard test case template, which means that the one which is decided for the project.

Review the test cases

Review the test case by giving it to the head of the team and, after that, fix the review feedback given by the reviewer.

Test case approval

After fixing the test case based on the feedback, send it again for approval.

Store in the test case repository

After the approval of the particular test case, store in the familiar place that is known as the test case repository.

Test case review process

Test Case Review process / Peer review process :

Customer gives requirements – development team starts developing the product looking at the requirements – testing team starts writing test cases looking at the requirements. Test engineers (you) are writing test cases for a particular module based on the requirements. Once all the possible test cases have been written for that particular module, you send a mail to the Test lead saying that you have finished writing test cases for that module. Now, what the test lead does is – he tells someone in the same testing team to review your test cases. The reviewer reviews all your test cases looking at your module's requirements and in case of any mistakes sends it to you and also to your test lead. You correct all the mistakes and send a copy of the corrected test cases both to the test lead and to the reviewer. It need not be that all mistakes pointed out by the reviewer be correct, if you feel they are wrong, then you need to give proper justification as to why your test cases are correct. Once the reviewer says all the test cases are fine, he sends a mail to the test lead saying all the test cases are fine. The test lead then approves your test cases and sends an approval mail to you saying that all the test cases are fine and to start executing the test cases.

While reviewing, the reviewer checks the following,

1) Template – he checks whether the template is as per decided for the project

2) Header :

a) Checks whether all the attributes are captured or not

b) Checks whether all the attributes in the header are filled or not

c) Checks whether all the attributes in the header are relevant or not

3) Body :

a) Check whether all possible scenarios are covered or not

b) Check whether the flow of test case is good or not

c) Check whether the test case design techniques are applied or not

d) The test cases should be organized in such a way that it should less time to execute

e) Check whether the test case is simple to understand and execute

f) Check whether proper navigation steps is written or not

Once test cases are reviewed, the review comments should not be sent via email or in notepad.

When the test engineer writes a test case, he/she may skip some scenarios, inputs and writes wrong navigation steps, which may affect the entire test execution process.

To avoid this, we will do one round of **review and approval process** before starting test execution.

If we don't go for the review process, we **miss out some scenarios, accuracy won't be there, and the test engineer won't be serious.**

All the cases need to be sent for the review process only after the completion of writing the test case. So, the other person does not get disturbed.

Once the author finishes writing the test case, it needs to be sent for the other test engineer known as a **reviewer** for the review process.

The reviewer opens the test case with the corresponding requirement and checks the **correctness of the test case, proper flow, and maximum test coverage**.

During this review process, if the reviewer found any mistake, he/she writes it in a separate document, which is known as a Review **document** and sends it back to the author.

The author goes through all the review comments and starts doing the changes if it is necessary, then sends it back once again for the review process.

This correction process will continue until both authors, and the reviewer will satisfied.

Once the review is successful, the reviewer sends it back to the **test lead** for the final approval process.

During this approval process, the **Team leads** are always kept in the loop so that the author and reviewer will be serious in their jobs.

When the test cases are written, reviewed, and approved, it will be stored in one centralized location, which is known as the Test **Case Repository**.

Note:

Test Case Repository

- A test case repository is a centralized location where all the baseline test cases (written, reviewed, and approved) are stored.
- When the client gives the requirements, the developer starts developing the modules, and the test engineer will write the test cases according to the requirements.
- A test case repository is used to store the approved test cases.
- Any test engineer wants to test the application, then he/she needs to access the test case only from the test case repository.
- If we do not require any test case, we can drop them from the test case repository.
- For every release, we maintain a different test case repository.
- Once the test cases are baselined or stored in the test case repository, they cannot be edited or changed without the permission of the test lead.
- The testing team always has a complete back-up of the test case repository if any crash happens which is affecting the software.

Review Process

While reviewing, the reviewer checks the following aspect in the test cases:

Template

The reviewer checks whether the template is as per requirements for the product or not.

Header

In the header, we check the following aspects:

- All the attributes are captured or not.
- All the attributes are relevant or not.
- All the attributes are filled or not.

Body

In the body of the test case, we will check the following aspects:

- The test case should be prepared so that it should take minimum time for the execution process.
- All the possible scenarios are covered or not.
- Look for the flow including maximum test Coverage
- The test case design technique is applied or not.
- The test case should be simple to understand
- Proper navigation is written or not.

Once the test case is reviewed, the review comments will be sent to the test case review template.

The reviewer will use the above template and send the comments. If the author fixes the test case, he/she would report it as fixed.

Text Execution Report [Excel]

It is the final document, which is prepared by a test lead when the entire testing process is completed.

The test execution report defined the stability of the application and contained the information like the number of cases written, executed, pass, fail, and their percentage.

The test execution report is a final summary report based on which the quality of the application is defined, and it also helps in deciding that the application can be handed over to the customer or not.

Every module has a separate spreadsheet of their respective module.

Let see one example of a test execution report where we have different modules such as **Sales, Amount transfer, Tax, Loan**.

The test lead made this report, and the test engineer sends the individual features that he/she has tested and executed.

The test lead sends this report to the following:

- **Development Team**
- **Management**
- **Test manager**
- **Customer**

Where a development team needs the list of failed test cases.

As we can see in the below table that we have a list of test case names, related status, and comments.

The below table is showing the amount transfer test case data.

Amount Transfer

Test Scenario

The test scenario is a detailed document of test cases that cover end to end functionality of a software application in liner statements. The liner statement is considered as a scenario. The test scenario is a high-level classification of testable requirements. These requirements are grouped on the basis of the functionality of a module and obtained from the use cases.

In the test scenario, there is a detailed testing process due to many associated test cases. Before performing the test scenario, the tester has to consider the test cases for each scenario.

In the test scenario, testers need to put themselves in the place of the user because they test the software application under the user's point of view. Preparation of scenarios is the most critical part, and it is necessary to seek advice or help from customers, stakeholders or developers to prepare the scenario.

Note:

The test scenarios can never be used for the text execution process because it does not consist of navigation steps and input.

These are the high-level documents that talks about all the possible combination or multiple ways or combinations of using the application and the primary purpose of the test scenarios are to understand the overall flow of the application.

How to write Test Scenarios

As a tester, follow the following steps to create Test Scenarios-

- Read the requirement document such as BRS (Business Requirement Specification), SRS (System Requirement Specification) and FRS (Functional Requirement Specification) of the software which is under the test.
- Determine all technical aspects and objectives for each requirement.
- Find all the possible ways by which the user can operate the software.
- Ascertain all the possible scenarios due to which system can be misused and also detect the users who can be hackers.
- After reading the requirement document and completion of the scheduled analysis make a list of various test scenarios to verify each function of the software.
- Once you list all the possible test scenarios, create a traceability matrix to find out whether each and every requirement has a corresponding test scenario or not.
- Supervisor of the project reviews all scenarios. Later, they are evaluated by other stakeholders of the project.

Features of Test Scenario

- The test scenario is a liner statement that guides testers for the testing sequence.
- Test scenario reduces the complexity and repetition of the product.
- Test scenario means talking and thinking about tests in detail but writing them in liner statements.
- It is a thread of operations.
- Test scenarios become more important when the tester does not have enough time to write test cases, and team members agree with a detailed liner scenario.
- The test scenario is a time saver activity.
- It provides easy maintenance because the addition and modification of test scenarios are easy and independent.

Note:

Some rules have to be followed when we were writing test scenarios:

- Always list down the most commonly used feature and module by the users.
- We always start the scenarios by picking module by module so that a proper sequence is followed as well as we don't miss out on any module level.
- Generally, scenarios are module level.
- Delete scenarios should always be the last option else, and we will waste lots of time in creating the data once again.
- It should be written in a simple language.
- Every scenario should be written in one line or a maximum of two lines and not in the paragraphs.
- Every scenario should consist of Dos and checks.

Example of Test scenarios

Here we are taking the **Gmail application** and writing test scenarios for different modules which are most commonly used such as **Login, Compose, Inbox, and Trash**

Test scenarios on the Login module

- Enter the valid login details (Username, password), and check that the home page is displayed.
- Enter the invalid Username and password and check for the home page.
- Leave Username and password blank, and check for the error message displayed.
- Enter the valid Login, and click on the cancel, and check for the fields reset.
- Enter invalid Login, more than three times, and check that account is blocked.
- Enter valid Login, and check that the **Username** is displayed on the home screen.

Test scenarios on Compose module

- Checks that all users can enter email ides in the **To, Cc, and Bcc**.
- Check that the entire user can enter various email ids in To, Cc, and Bcc.
- Compose a mail, send it, and check for the confirmation message.
- Compose a mail, send it, and check in the sent item of the sender and the inbox.
- Compose a mail, send it, and check for invalid and valid email id (valid format), check the mail in sender inbox.
- Compose main, discard, and then check for confirmation message and check-in draft.
- Compose mail click on save as draft and check for the confirmation message
- Compose mail click on close and check for conformation save as drafts.

Test scenarios on Inbox module

- Click on the inbox, and verify all received mail are displayed and highlighted in the inbox.
- Check that the latest received mail has been displayed to the sender email id correctly.
- Select the mail, reply and forward send it; check in the sent item of sender and inbox of the receiver.
- Check for any attached attachments to the mail that are downloaded or not.
- Check that attachment is scanned correctly for any viruses before download.
- Select the mail, reply and forward save as draft, and check for the confirmation message and checks in the Draft section.
- Check all the emails are marked as read and are not highlighted.

- Check all mail recipients in **Cc** are visible to all users.
- Checks all email recipients in **Bcc** are not visible to the users.
- Select mail, delete it, and then check in the **Trash** section.

Test scenario on Trash module

- Open trash, check all deleted mail present.
- Restore mail from Trash; check-in the corresponding module.
- Select mail from trash, delete it, and check mail is permanently deleted.

What is Test Strategy?

A high-level document is used to validate the test types or levels to be executed for the product and specify the **Software Development Life Cycle's** testing approach is known as Test strategy document.

Once the test strategy has been written, we cannot modify it, and it is approved by the **Project Manager, development team.**

Manual Testing Interview Questions – FAQs

1. How do I prepare for a manual test interview?

To prepare for a manual testing interview, it is important to review the fundamentals of manual testing, understand different testing techniques, and practice with sample test cases. Additionally, familiarize yourself with common interview questions and be ready to discuss your experience and problem-solving skills.

2. What are the important questions in manual testing?

Important questions in manual testing can cover a range of topics, including *test case design, test execution, defect tracking, and test documentation*. Some common questions may include explaining the **difference between smoke testing and regression testing, discussing the importance of boundary value analysis, or describing the steps involved in the bug life cycle.**

3. What is manual testing in an interview?

In an interview, manual testing refers to the process of testing software applications manually, without the use of automated tools. It involves executing test cases, identifying defects, and verifying that the software meets the specified requirements. Interviewers may ask about your understanding of manual testing concepts, methodologies, and best practices.

4. What are the skills for manual testing?

Skills required for manual testing include a strong understanding of software testing concepts, knowledge of different testing techniques, attention to detail, analytical thinking, and good communication skills. Additionally, proficiency in test case design, bug tracking, and test documentation is important. Familiarity with testing tools and the ability to work well in a team are also valuable skills for manual testers.

In this section, we have compiled the most frequently asked manual software testing questions for freshers. So, if you are a newbie in the [software testing](#) world, then explore this section to know what types of questions you will face during the software tester job profile

1. What is Manual Software Testing?

Manual Testing is a type of software testing process where test cases are executed manually without using any automated tool.

- The tester verifies the software functionality manually.
- The tester has a list of all the test cases that need to be manually tested. They go through each test case and manually verify the output.
- It is inefficient in comparison to automated testing, slow, and not repeatable in a consistent manner.
- Manual testing is prone to human misjudgment.

2. What are the Advantages of Manual Testing?

- **Better for Short-Lifecycle Projects:** Manual testing is better for projects with short life cycles.
- **Time and cost-efficiency:** It is better to opt for manual testing for small, easy projects to save time, money, and resources.
- **A good** product-oriented **option for GUI testing:** Manual testing can be done accurately for GUI Testing.
- **Easy to learn:** It is easy to learn for new testers.
- **Uses human intelligence:** Manual testing allows testers to use their higher cognitive abilities to detect errors. This helps them to find errors that may be missed during automated testing.
- **Detect errors outside the code:** Manual testing helps testers to locate bugs that do not affect the code such as server response time.

3. What are the Drawbacks of Manual Testing?

- **Time-consuming:** Manual testing requires time as the tester executes test cases manually and testing complex programs could take some time.
- **Human error:** Manual testing is prone to human error. By making mistakes when executing test cases, testers may come up with erroneous results.
- **Difficult to measure:** It is difficult to assess the efficiency of the manual testing process as it is difficult to keep track of the quality of the test cases executed, errors discovered, and test coverage attained.
- **Costly:** Manual testing can be expensive, particularly for big, complex projects, or when frequent releases are required.

4. List key challenges of Manual Testing.

Below are some of the key challenges of manual testing:

- **Lack of standard documentation:** Lack of standard documentation to understand the application fully to have a better insight into the application makes it difficult for the tester to create test cases for manual testing efficiently.
- **Unavailability of skilled testers:** Manual testing depends on Human intelligence, and analytical skills to design test cases that can ensure the best coverage.
- **Deciding test cases order:** It is very important to prioritize, and categorize the test cases and decide the order in which to execute the test cases.
- **Ability to know when to stop testing: A tester needs to have product-oriented** knowledge and the ability to decide when to stop testing the application to save time and effort.

5. How Manual Testing is different from Automated Testing?

Manual testing is a software testing process in which a tester tests each test case one by one in an individual manner. Whereas in automated testing, the tester utilizes tools and scripts to automate testing efforts.

Parameters

Manual Testing

Automated Testing

Definition

In manual testing, **the tester executes test cases manually.**

In automated testing, the tester uses tools and scripts to automate the process of testing.

Working

Manual testing works by requiring analysts and QA engineers to be involved in everything right from test case creation to actual test execution.

Automated testing involves testers writing test scripts that automate test case execution.

Strength

Manual testing is better at handling complex scenarios.

Automated testing is much faster and covers many permutations.

Weakness

Manual testing is slow and tedious.

Automated testing requires coding and test maintenance.

Test coverage

It isn't easy to ensure sufficient test coverage.

It is easy to ensure sufficient test coverage.

6. Who is a Manual Tester?

The manual tester is a professional who is responsible for conducting quality checks on the software applications without using **automation tools**. They are responsible for manually checking the software for errors and fixing them. They must have appropriate skills to be able to meet the company's requirements.

7. What is the role of documentation in Manual Testing?

Documentation plays a vital role in manual testing. It is important to document all steps taken in the testing process to ensure sufficient test coverage and accurate results. It provides an audit trail, which can be used to evaluate past test results and identify areas of improvement. It also serves as a reference for other testers who may be unfamiliar with the system.

8. What are the Priority and Severity in Software Testing?

Priority is the order in which the developer should resolve the defect, on the other hand, Severity is the degree of impact that defect has on the operation of the product.

- Priority indicates how soon the bug is fixed and severity shows the seriousness of the defect on the product functionality.
- Priority is driven by the business values and Severity is driven by the functionality of the product.

9. What is Test Harness?

Test Harness is a collection of stubs, drivers, and other supporting tools that are required to automate the test execution. It executes tests using a test library and generates test reports.

- It helps automate the testing procedures and thus increases the productivity of the system through automation.
- A test harness is a collection of numerous things to test software and report its results.
- It helps developers to measure the cove coverage at a code level.

10. What is a Test Bed?

Test Bed is a test execution environment that is configured for testing. It consists of specific hardware, software, **operating system**, network configuration, other system software, and application software.

11. What is test data?

Test data is data that is used by test cases to determine if the software is working correctly or not. It is collected into a document known as a test data document so that testers can easily access it when they run their tests.

12. What is Quality Control(QC) in testing?

Quality Control is a set of methods that are used by the organization to ensure the quality of software by identifying defects and correcting defects in the developed software.

- It provides the identification of defects.
- It is product-oriented.
- It is a reactive process.
- The testing team is responsible for Quality Control.

13. What is Test Closure?

Test closure is a document that provides a summary of all the tests covered during the [software development lifecycle](#).

- It includes various activities like test completion reporting, a summary of test results as well and the test completion matrix.
- It gives us an outline of the tests conducted during the software testing and details of the errors and bugs found and resolved during the testing phase.

14. What is Random Testing?

Random testing also known as Monkey Testing is a type of software testing in which the system is tested with the help of generating random and independent inputs and test cases.

- It is performed where the defects are not identified at regular intervals.
- It saves time and effort more than actual test efforts.

Manual Testing Questions for Intermediate

In this section, we have compiled the top manual testing interview questions for intermediate. So if you have one or two years of experience, then this section is totally for these types of software testers.

15. What is Defect Cascading?

Defect cascading in software testing means when one defect leads to the discovery of other defects. It often occurs because the original defect was not fixed properly. This cascading causes a chain reaction of errors, making it difficult to source the problem.

- It can lead to many issues like minor performance slowdowns, system crashes, etc making it a severe risk to developers and testers.
- Understanding defect cascading can help to prevent them from happening in their process.

16. What is a Test Driver?

Test drivers are used in Bottom-up integration testing to simulate the behavior of the upper-level modules that are not yet integrated.

- They act as temporary replacements for a calling module.

- They give the same output as that of the actual product.
- They are used when the software needs to interact with an external system and are usually more complex than stubs.

17. What is a Stub?

Stubs are used in Top-Down integration testing thus increasing the efficiency of the testing process.

- They are developed by software developers to use them in place of modules, if the respective modules are not developed, missing in the developing stage, or currently unavailable.
- It simulates a module that has all the capabilities of the unavailable module.

18. What is Defect Triage?

Defect triage is a procedure that involves detecting and prioritizing problems, allocating them to development, and tracking them.

- The goal is to evaluate, prioritize, and assign the resolution of defects.
- It is also known as bug triage.
- It is based on the severity and priority of the defects in software.

19. What is API Testing?

[API testing](#) is a type of software testing that validates APIs. It aims to check the functionality, reliability, performance, and security of the programming interfaces.

- It verifies that the API returns the correct response for different input values.
- It ensures that the different components of a system can communicate with each other correctly and that the system can handle a large volume of requests.

20. What is Alpha Testing?

Alpha Testing is a type of software testing performed to identify bugs before releasing the product to real users or the public. It is one of the user acceptance tests that is done near the end of the development of the software.

- It is generally performed by the homestead software engineers or quality assurance staff.
- It is used to identify and resolve critical bugs and issues in the software before it is released to the public.
- It is performed in a controlled environment like a lab or a test network and is used to simulate real-world use cases.

21. What is Beta Testing?

Beta testing is the process of testing a software product or service in a real-world environment before its official release. It helps identify bugs and errors that may have been missed during the development process.

- During beta testing, the software is made available to a selected group of users who are willing to test the product and provide feedback to the developers.
- The beta testers typically use the software in various ways, attempting to find any issues, bugs, or usability problems.
- They then provide feedback on their experience, reporting any problems or issues encountered.

22. What are the types of Manual Testing?

Manual testing is of the following different types:

1. **Black box testing:** Black box testing is a software testing method that focuses on testing the functionality of the software without dealing with the internal structures or workings.
2. **White box testing:** White box testing is a software testing method that tests the internal structure of the application as opposed to its functionality.
3. **Unit testing:** Unit testing is a software testing method in which the smallest testable parts of the application called units are tested for proper operation.
4. **System testing:** System testing is a software testing method in which the QA team e
5. valuates how the various components of an application interact together in a fully integrated system.
6. **Integration testing:** Integration testing is a type of software testing method in which different modules or units of a software application are tested as a combined entity.
7. **Acceptance testing:** Acceptance testing is a type of software testing method that is performed after system testing and before making the system available for actual use.

23. List the roles and responsibilities of Manual testers.

Below are some of the roles and responsibilities of Manual Tester:

1. Analyzing client requirements.
2. Reviewing written code for compliance with project specifications and requirements.
3. Creating a test environment for executing the test cases.
4. Organizing and conducting review meetings.
5. Detecting and fixing bugs.
6. Monitor system errors and discuss them with the team.

24. Describe Manual Testing Process.

Manual testing is a process of identifying bugs and errors in software without the use of automated tools. Below is the process of manual testing:

1. **Identify the scope of testing:** The first step is to identify the scope of testing and the scope can vary from a functionality to an end-to-end system.
2. **Design test cases:** The next step is to design test cases including test scenarios, data, expected results, and all other details that are necessary to perform the tests on the identified scope.

3. **Execute test cases:** After designing the test cases, testers execute the test cases to find the discrepancies between the actual result and the expected result.
4. **Record results:** Testers should record the results for further analysis.

25. What are the different levels of Manual Testing?

Different levels of Manual Testing are:

1. **Unit Testing:** Unit testing is a process of testing the individual pieces of code within the system called units. The main focus is on the functional accuracy of the standalone modules.
2. **Integration Testing:** Integration testing involves combining and testing the individual units to see if they work together as expected or not.
3. **System Testing:** System testing involves testing all the components of the product as a whole to ensure that overall product requirements are met or not.
4. **User Acceptance Testing:** User Acceptance Testing is the final step in the testing process that determines if the software is ready for release or not.

26. What are the Skills required for Manual Testing?

Some of the important skills required for manual testing are:

- A strong analytical ability.
- Ability to report test results professionally.
- Familiarity with agile methodologies.
- Ability to write test cases for manual testing.
- Knowledge of concepts required for manual testing like SDLC, STLC, SQL, etc.
- Understanding of manual testing tools like JIRA, JMeter, etc.
- Understanding of test management tools and test tracking tools.

27. When to use Manual Testing over Automation Testing?

There are many scenarios when manual testing can be opted over automation testing in a project:

- **Adhoc Testing:** Adhoc testing can be achieved using manual testing as there is not no specific approach and is performed without planning and documentation. In ad hoc testing the understanding and insight of the tester plays an important role.
- **Exploratory test:** Exploratory testing depends upon the tester's knowledge, experience, and logical skills, so human involvement is a must here and manual testing is the best choice for exploratory tests.
- **Usability testing:** In Usability testing human observation plays a very important role as it is measured by the tester how user-friendly, and efficient the software is for the end users. So manual testing is an appropriate choice for usability testing.
- **Short lifecycle projects:** Automation testing is not appropriate for short-term projects as it requires high investment and planning and manual testing on the other hand aims to save time and resources.

28. What are Manual Testing Tools?

Manual testing is a software testing method in which the tester manually executes the test cases without the use of automated technologies. The tools that help in this process are known as manual testing tools. Some examples of manual testing tools are Bugzilla, JMeter, JIRA, etc.

Manual Testing Interview Questions for Experienced

This section contains manual testing interview questions for experienced. So, if you have years of experience and are looking for change, then explore this section. Here you will find all the interview questions for the software testing experience profile.

29. List some Manual Testing Tools.

Below are some of the commonly used Manual Testing tools:

1. **Trac:** Trac is one of the most powerful manual testing tools that is developed in Python and is a web-based program. It is compatible with a variety of databases like [SQLite](), [MySQL](), MS-SQL, etc.
2. **TestLink:** TestLink is a high-quality product that has more functions in a comparable package. It is simple to use as the program is available to use through a browser.
3. **JMeter:** JMeter is an open-source tool for performance testing of static and dynamic resources and dynamic web applications. It has an easy-to-use and clear interface accepting JVMs from Windows, Mac OS X, Linux, and other platforms.
4. **Bugzilla:** Bugzilla is an open-source application that helps customers and clients to keep track of issues. It has a simple-to-use Google-style bug search that also searches the complete text of a bug.
5. **Load Runner:** It is the most commonly used performance testing tool that is used to categorize the most prevalent causes of performance problems rapidly. It is compatible with a variety of development tools and protocol stacks and it helps to lower the cost of distributed load testing.

30. What are the best practices for writing test cases for Manual Testing?

Below are some of the best practices that can be followed for writing the test cases:

- **Prioritize test cases:** Prioritize which test cases to build based on the application's risk considerations and project timeframes.
- **Follow the 80/20 rule:** To ensure sufficient coverage, it is better to have 20% of the test cases cover 80% of the application.
- **Categorize test cases:** List all the test cases and categorize the test cases according to business scenarios and functionality.
- **Design modular test cases:** Make sure that the test cases are modular and as detailed as possible.
- **Remove duplicate test cases:** Remove irrelevant and duplicate test cases.

31. Can Automation Testing replace Manual Testing?

Automation testing cannot completely replace Manual testing as it is not possible to automate everything. Manual testing can be used in situations where automation isn't possible. Both automated and manual testing have their advantages and disadvantages.

32. List the differences between the Test Case and Test Scenario.

Test Case	Test Scenario
A test case is a detailed document that provides details about the testing strategy, testing process, preconditions, and expected output	A test scenario gives one-line information about what to test and is derived from the use case.
These are low-level actions.	These are high-level actions.
The purpose is to verify the test scenario by implementing the steps	The purpose of the test scenario is to cover the end-to-end functionality of software functionality.
It takes more time.	It takes less time.
It can be obtained from test scenarios.	It can be obtained from the use case.

33. What is Smoke Testing?

Smoke testing also known as Build Verification Testing is a software testing method that is performed at the beginning of the development process to make sure that the most critical functions of the software applications are working correctly.

- It is done to quickly identify and fix the major issues before more detailed testing is performed.
- The goal is to determine whether the build is stable enough to proceed with further testing.

34. What is Regression Testing?

Regression testing is a software testing process of testing previously tested programs to ensure that the defects have not been introduced or uncovered in unchanged areas of the software as a result of the changes made in the software.

35. List the differences between Sanity Testing and Smoke Testing.

Sanity Testing	Smoke Testing
Sanity testing is performed to check whether the new functionality/ bug has been fixed.	Smoke testing is performed to make sure that the critical functionality of the system is working correctly.

The goal of sanity testing is to verify rationality.	The goal of smoke testing is to verify stability.
Sanity testing isn't documented.	Smoke testing is documented.
Testers perform sanity testing.	Software developers or testers perform smoke testing.
The software build is relatively stable at the time of sanity testing.	The software build may be either stable or unstable during smoke testing.

36. What is Top-Down Integration Testing?

Top-down integration Testing is an Integration testing technique in which testing is done by integrating two or more modules by moving down from top to bottom through the control flow of the architecture structure.

- High-level modules are tested first and then the low-level modules are tested.
- Stubs are the modules that act as temporary replacements for the called module.

37. List the differences between Regression and Retesting.

Regression	Retesting
Regression testing is done to ensure that the changes have not affected the unchanged part of the product.	Retesting is done to ensure that the test cases which failed in the last execution are fixed.
The purpose of regression testing is to check that the new code changes should not have any side effects on the existing functionalities.	The purpose of retesting is to check whether the functionality has been restored following a bug fix.
Automating regression testing is possible as Manual testing can be time-consuming and expensive.	Automating test cases for retesting is not possible.

Regression testing is done for passed test cases.	Retesting is done for failed test cases.
Defect Verification is not part of regression testing.	Defect Verification is part of retesting.

38. List some Test Management Tools.

1. **QACoverage:** QACoverage is a test management tool that is cost-effective, boosts test productivity, and provides visibility to better handle the QA process. It provides the ability to upload 1000 requirements and test cases from Excel spreadsheets in seconds and supports complete traceability between requirements, test cases, and defects.
2. **TestRail:** TestRail is a web-based test case management tool that helps teams organize testing efforts and get real-time insights into testing activity. It helps to capture details about test cases with screenshots and expected results. It is possible to compare results across multiple test runs, configurations, and milestones.
3. **SpiraTest:** SpiraTest is a test management tool from Infectra that helps agile teams deliver high-quality software faster and with greater confidence. It helps users manage all their tests, requirements, and bugs in one place. It allows for easy importing of data from many modern applications.
4. **Testiny:** Testiny is a test management tool that aims to make manual testing and QA management as seamless as possible. It helps testers perform tests without adding bulky overhead to the testing process.
5. **TestMonitor:** TestMonitor is an end-to-end test management tool that supports advanced test case design capable of supporting thousands of cases. It supports comprehensive result tracking and smart reporting with many filter and visualization options.

39. What is the Bug Life Cycle?

Bug life cycle also known as Defect Life Cycle is the life cycle of a defect or bug from which it goes through covering a specific set of states in its entire life. The below diagram illustrates the actual workflow of the Defect Life Cycle:

The above diagram shows different states of Defect in the Defect Life Cycle and these are as follows :

1. **New:** When any new defect is identified by the tester, it falls into a 'New' state. It is the first state of the Bug Life Cycle.
2. **Assigned:** Defects that are in the status of 'New' will be approved and that newly identified defect will be assigned to the development team to work on the defect and resolve that.
3. **Open:** In this 'Open' state the defect is being addressed by the developer team and the developer team works on the defect for fixing the bug. Based on some specific reason if the developer team feels that the defect is not appropriate then it is transferred to either the 'Rejected' or �rred' state.

4. **Fixed:** After necessary changes of codes or after fixing the identified bug developer team marks the state as '???? ixed'.
5. **Pending Retest:** During the fixing of the defect is completed, the developer team passes new code to the testing team for a retest. The code/application is pending for retesting at the Tester side so the status is assigned as 'Pending Retest'.
6. **Retest:** At this stage, the tester starts work of retesting the defect to check whether the defect is fixed by the developer or not, and the status is marked as 'Retesting'.
7. **Reopen:** After 'Retesting' if the tester team finds that the bug continues like previously even after the developer team has fixed the bug, then the status of the bug is again changed to 'Reopened'. Once again bug goes to the 'Open' state and goes through the life cycle again. This means it goes for Re-fixing by the developer team.
8. **Verified:** The tester re-tests the bug after it got fixed by the developer team and if the tester does not find any kind of defect/bug then the bug is fixed and the status assigned is 'Verified'.
9. **Closed:** It is the final state of the Defect Cycle, after fixing the defect by the developer team when testing found that the bug had been resolved and did not persist they marked the defect as a '???? lost' state.

40. List some Bug Tracking Tools.

1. **JIRA:** One of the most essential bug-tracking tools is Jira. Jira is an open-source platform used in manual testing for bug tracking, project management, and problem tracking. Jira contains a variety of capabilities such as reporting, recording, and workflow. We can monitor all types of faults and issues connected to software that is created by the test engineer in Jira.
2. **BugHerd:** BugHerd is the simplest way to monitor issues, collect feedback, and manage web page feedback. It also saves information like the browser, CSS selector data, operating system, and even a screenshot to help quickly recreate and fix errors. It is the most user-friendly tool for tracking problems and managing website feedback.
3. **Bugzilla:** Bugzilla is an open-source program that is used to assist the customer and client in keeping track of issues. It is also used as a test management tool since it allows us to quickly connect other test case management solutions such as ALM, Quality Centre, and so on.
4. **Axosoft:** Axosoft is a bug-tracking solution that may be used with hosted or on-premises applications. It is a Scrum team project management tool.
5. **Backlog:** Backlog is a web-based error/bug tracking and project management application designed for software development teams. The tool comes with a variety of features, including subtasks and detailed status charts, as well as iOS and Android apps.

41. List the differences between Quality Assurance (QA) and Quality Control (QC).

Quality Assurance	Quality Control
QA is a group of activities that ensures that the quality of processes used during	QC is a group of activities to detect defects in the developed software.

software development is always maintained.	
QA focuses on assuring that the quality requested will be achieved.	QC focuses on fulfilling the quality request
QA is process-oriented.	QC is product-oriented.
QA is a managerial tool.	QC is a corrective tool.
Verification	Validation

42. What is Pesticide Paradox?

Pesticide paradox means if the same tests are repeated over and over again then the same test cases will no longer find new bugs. Some of the methods to prevent pesticide paradoxes are to write a whole new set of test cases to exercise different parts of the software or to prepare new test cases and add them to the existing test cases.

43. What is a Critical Bug?

A critical bug is a bug that tends to affect the majority of the functionality of the given application or software. The software cannot be released unless the critical bug is addressed.

44. What makes a good test engineer?

A good test engineer should have the following traits:

- Detail Oriented and organized.
- Has excellent problem-solving skills.
- Has strong communication and collaboration skills.
- A good test engineer must be up to date on the latest technologies.

45. List the differences between Alpha testing and Beta testing.

Alpha Testing	Beta Testing
Alpha Testing is a type of software testing performed to identify bugs before releasing the product to real users or the public.	Beta testing is the process of testing a software product or service in a real-world environment before its official release.
Alpha testing is performed by testers who are usually employees of the organization.	Beta testing is performed by clients who are not part of the organization.
Alpha testing involves both white box and black box testing.	Beta testing involves black box testing.
Reliability and security testing are not checked in alpha testing.	Reliability, security, and robustness are checked during beta testing
Alpha testing requires a testing environment or lab.	Reliability, security, and robustness are checked during beta testing.

Real-Time Interview Questions on Manual Testing

46. How many test cases can be executed in a day in Manual Testing?

It depends upon the test case complexity and the size. Some test cases have few steps and some have more test steps.

47. How do you derive test cases?

It depends upon the project, sometimes we derive test cases from requirements and sometimes from use cases.

48. How much time is required to write a test case?

This depends upon the complexity of the software project.

49. Were you involved in Test plan documentation in your career?

Yes, I was involved in test plan documentation in my last project. I have identified Entry criteria, exit criteria, features to be tested, etc.

50. Why did you choose Software Testing as a career?

I would love to be a Software tester because I love solving puzzles and testing is like solving a puzzle, not only finding bugs but breaking into the system through stress testing

A list of mostly asked **software testing interview questions** or **QTP interview questions** and answers are given below.

1) What is the PDCA cycle and where testing fits in?

There are four steps in a normal software development process. In short, these steps are referred to as PDCA.

PDCA stands for Plan, Do, Check, Act.

- **Plan:** It defines the goal and the plan for achieving that goal.
- **Do/ Execute:** It depends on the plan strategy decided during the planning stage. It is done according to this phase.
- **Check:** This is the testing part of the software development phase. It is used to ensure that we are moving according to plan and getting the desired result.
- **Act:** This step is used to solve if there any issue has occurred during the check cycle. It takes appropriate action accordingly and revises the plan again.

The developers do the "planning and building" of the project while testers do the "check" part of the project.

2) What is the difference between the white box, black box, and gray box testing?

Black box Testing: The strategy of black box testing is based on requirements and specification. It requires no knowledge of internal path, structure or implementation of the software being tested.

White box Testing: White box testing is based on internal paths, code structure, and implementation of the software being tested. It requires a full and detailed programming skill.

Gray box Testing: This is another type of testing in which we look into the box which is being tested, It is done only to understand how it has been implemented. After that, we close the box and use the black box testing.

Following are the differences among white box, black box, and gray box testing are:

Black Box Testing	White Box Testing	Grey Box Testing
Black box testing does not need the implementation knowledge of a program.	In white box testing, implementation details of a program are fully required.	Gray box testing knows the limited knowledge of an internal program.
It has a low granularity.	It has a high granularity.	It has a medium granularity.
It is also known as opaque box testing, closed box testing, input-output testing, data-driven testing, behavioral testing and functional testing.	It is also known as glass box testing, clear box testing.	It is also known as translucent testing.
It is a user acceptance testing, i.e., it is done by end users.	Testers and programmers mainly do it.	Test cases are made by the internal details of a program.
Test cases are made by the functional specifications as internal details are not known.	Test cases are made by the internal details of a program.	Test cases are made by the internal details of a program.

3) What are the advantages of designing tests early in the life cycle?

Designing tests early in the life cycle prevents defects from being in the main code.

4) What are the types of defects?

There are three types of defects: Wrong, missing, and extra.

Wrong: These defects have occurred due to requirements that have been implemented incorrectly.

Missing: It is used to specify the missing things, i.e., a specification was not implemented, or the requirement of the customer was not appropriately noted.

Extra: This is an extra facility incorporated into the product that was not given by the end customer. It is always a variance from the specification but may be an attribute that was desired by the customer. However, it is considered as a defect because of the variance from the user requirements.

5) What is exploratory testing?

Simultaneous test design and execution against an application is called exploratory testing. In this testing, the tester uses his domain knowledge and testing experience to predict where and under what conditions the system might behave unexpectedly.

6) When should exploratory testing be performed?

Exploratory testing is performed as a final check before the software is released. It is a complementary activity to automated regression testing.

7) What are the advantages of designing tests early in the life cycle?

It helps you to prevent defects in the code.

8) Tell me about the risk-based testing.

The risk-based testing is a testing strategy that is based on prioritizing tests by risks. It is based on a detailed risk analysis approach which categorizes the risks by their priority. Highest priority risks are resolved first.

9) What is acceptance testing?

Acceptance testing is done to enable a user/customer to determine whether to accept a software product. It also validates whether the software follows a set of agreed acceptance criteria. At this level, the system is tested for user acceptability.

Types of acceptance testing are:

1. **User acceptance testing**: It is also known as end-user testing. This type of testing is performed after the product is tested by the testers. The user acceptance testing is testing performed concerning the user needs, requirements, and business processes to determine whether the system satisfies the acceptance criteria or not.
2. **Operational acceptance testing**: An operational acceptance testing is performed before the product is released in the market. But, it is performed after the user acceptance testing.
3. **Contract and regulation acceptance testing**: In the case of contract acceptance testing, the system is tested against certain criteria and the criteria are made in a contract. In the case of regulation acceptance testing, the software application is checked whether it meets the government regulations or not.
4. **Alpha and beta testing**: Alpha testing is performed in the development environment before it is released to the customer. Input is taken from the alpha testers, and then the developer fixes the bug to improve the quality of a product. Unlike alpha testing, beta testing is performed in the customer environment. Customer performs the testing and provides the feedback, which is then implemented to improve the quality of a product.

10) What is accessibility testing?

Accessibility testing is used to verify whether a software product is accessible to the people having disabilities (deaf, blind, mentally disabled etc.).

11) What is Adhoc testing?

Ad-hoc testing is a testing phase where the tester tries to 'break' the system by randomly trying the system's functionality.

12) What is Agile testing?

Agile testing is a testing practice that uses agile methodologies i.e. follow test-first design paradigm.

13) What is API (Application Programming Interface)?

Application Programming Interface is a formalized set of software calls and routines that can be referenced by an application program to access supporting system or network services.

14) What do you mean by automated testing?

Testing by using software tools which execute tests without manual intervention is known as automated testing. Automated testing can be used in GUI, performance, API, etc.

15) What is Bottom-up testing?

Bottom-up testing is a testing approach which follows integration testing where the lowest level components are tested first, after that the higher level components are tested. The process is repeated until the testing of the top-level component.

16) What is Baseline Testing?

In Baseline testing, a set of tests is run to capture performance information. Baseline testing improves the performance and capabilities of the application by using the information collected and making the changes in the application. Baseline compares the present performance of the application with its previous performance.

17) What is Benchmark Testing?

Benchmarking testing is the process of comparing application performance with respect to the industry standard given by some other organization.

It is a standard testing which specifies where our application stands with respect to others.

18) Which types are testing are important for web testing?

There are two types of testing which are very important for web testing:

- **Performance testing**: Performance testing is a testing technique in which quality attributes of a system are measured such as responsiveness, speed under different load conditions and scalability. The performance testing describes which attributes need to be improved before the product is released in the market.
- **Security testing**: Security testing is a testing technique which determines that the data and resources be saved from the intruders.

19) What is the difference between web application and desktop application in the scenario of testing?

The difference between a web application and desktop application is that a web application is open to the world with potentially many users accessing the application simultaneously at various times, so load testing and stress testing are important. Web applications are also prone to all forms of attacks, mostly DDOS, so security testing is also very important in the case of web applications.

20) What is the difference between verification and validation?

Verification	Validation
Verification is Static Testing.	Validation is Dynamic Testing.

Verification occurs before Validation.	Validation occurs after Verification.
Verification evaluates plans, document, requirements and specification.	Validation evaluates products
In verification, inputs are the checklist, issues list, walkthroughs, and inspection.	Invalidation testing, the actual product is tested.
Verification output is a set of documents, plans, specification and requirement documents.	Invalidation of the actual product is output.

21) What is the difference between Retesting and Regression Testing?

Retesting	Regression
Retesting is the process of testing that checks the test cases which were failed in the final execution.	Regression is a type of software testing that checks the code change does not affect the current features and functions of an application.
Retesting is applied on the defect fixes.	The main purpose of regression testing is that the changes made to the code should not affect the existing functionalities.
Defect verification is an element of regression testing.	Defect verification is not an element of Regression testing.
Automation cannot be performed for Retesting.	Automation can be performed for regression testing while manual testing could be expensive and time-consuming.
Retesting is also known as planned testing.	Regression testing is also known as generic testing.

| Regression testing can be performed in parallel with the retesting. Priority of retesting is higher than the regression testing. | Regression testing concern with executing test cases that was passed in earlier builds. Retesting concern with executing those test cases that are failed earlier. |

22) What is the difference between preventative and reactive approaches to testing?

Preventative tests are designed earlier, and reactive tests are designed after the software has been produced.

23) What is the purpose of exit criteria?

The exit criteria are used to define the completion of the test level.

24) Why is decision table testing used?

A decision table consists of inputs in a column with the outputs in the same column but below the inputs.

The decision table testing is used for testing systems for which the specification takes the form of rules or cause-effect combination. The reminders you get in the table explore combinations of inputs to define the output produced.

25) What is alpha and beta testing?

These are the key differences between alpha and beta testing:

No.Alpha TestingBeta Testing1)It is always done by developers at the software development site.It is always performed by customers at their site.2)It is also performed by Independent testing teamIt is not be performed by Independent testing team3)It is not open to the market and public.It is open to the market and public.4)It is always performed in a virtual environment.It is always performed in a real-time environment.5)It is used for software applications and projects.It is used for software products.6)It follows the category of both white box testing and Black Box Testing.It is only the kind of Black Box Testing.7)It is not known by any other name.It is also known as field testing.

26) What is Random/Monkey Testing?

Random testing is also known as monkey testing. In this testing, data is generated randomly often using a tool. The data is generated either using a tool or some automated mechanism.

Random testing has some limitations:

- Most of the random tests are redundant and unrealistic.
- It needs more time to analyze results.
- It is not possible to recreate the test if you do not record what data was used for testing.

27) What is the negative and positive testing?

Negative Testing: When you put an invalid input and receive errors is known as negative testing.

Positive Testing: When you put in the valid input and expect some actions that are completed according to the specification is known as positive testing.

28) What is the benefit of test independence?

Test independence is very useful because it avoids author bias in defining effective tests.

29) What is boundary value analysis/testing?

In boundary value analysis/testing, we only test the exact boundaries rather than hitting in the middle. For example: If there is a bank application where you can withdraw a maximum of 25000 and a minimum of 100. So in boundary value testing we only test above the max and below the max. This covers all scenarios.

The following figure shows the boundary value testing for the above-discussed bank application.TC1 and TC2 are sufficient to test all conditions for the bank. TC3 and TC4 are duplicate/redundant test cases which do not add any value to the testing. So by applying proper boundary value fundamentals, we can avoid duplicate test cases, which do not add value to the testing.

30) How would you test the login feature of a web application?

There are many ways to test the login feature of a web application:

- Sign in with valid login, Close browser and reopen and see whether you are still logged in or not.
- Sign in, then log out and then go back to the login page to see if you are truly logged out.
- Log in, then go back to the same page, do you see the login screen again?
- Session management is important. You must focus on how do we keep track of logged in users, is it via cookies or web sessions?
- Sign in from one browser, open another browser to see if you need to sign in again?
- Log in, change the password, and then log out, then see if you can log in again with the old password.

31) What are the types of performance testing?

Performance testing: Performance testing is a testing technique which determines the performance of the system such as speed, scalability, and stability under various load conditions. The product undergoes the performance testing before it gets live in the market.

Types of software testing are:

1. Load testing:

- Load testing is a testing technique in which a system is tested with an increasing load until it reaches the threshold value.

Note: An increasing load means the increasing number of users.

- The main purpose of load testing is to check the response time of the system with an increasing amount of load.
- Load testing is non-functional testing means that the only non-functional requirements are tested.
- Load testing is performed to make sure that the system can withstand a heavy load

2. Stress testing:

- Stress testing is a testing technique to check the system when hardware resources are not enough such as CPU, memory, disk space, etc.
- In case of stress testing, software is tested when the system is loaded with the number of processes and the hardware resources are less.
- The main purpose of stress testing is to check the failure of the system and to determine how to recover from this failure is known as recoverability.
- Stress testing is non-functional testing means that the only non-functional requirements are tested.

3. Spike testing:

- Spike testing is a subset of load testing. This type of testing checks the instability of the application when the load is varied.
- There are different cases to be considered during testing:
  - The first case is not to allow the number of users so that the system will not suffer heavy load.
  - The second case is to provide warnings to the extra joiners, and this would slow down the response time.

4. Endurance testing:

- Endurance testing is a subset of load testing. This type of testing checks the behavior of the system.

- Endurance testing is non-functional testing means that the only non-functional requirements are tested.
- Endurance testing is also known as Soak testing.
- Endurance testing checks the issues such as memory leak. A memory leak occurs when the program does not release its allocated memory after its use. Sometimes the application does not release its memory even after its use and this unusable memory causes memory leak. This causes an issue when the application runs for a long duration.
- Some of the main issues that are viewed during this testing are:
    - Memory leaks occurred due to an application.
    - Memory leaks occurred due to a database connection.
    - Memory leaks occurred due to a third party software.

5. Volume testing:

- Volume testing is a testing technique in which the system is tested when the volume of data is increased.
- Volume testing is also known as flood testing.
- Volume testing is non-functional testing means that the only non-functional requirements are tested.
- For example: If we want to apply volume testing then we need to expand the database size, i.e., add more data into the database table and then perform the test.

6. Scalability testing

- Scalability testing is a testing technique that ensures that the system works well in proportion to the growing demands of the end users.
- Following are the attributes checked during this testing:
    - Response time
    - Throughput
    - Number of users required for performance test
    - Threshold load
    - CPU usage
    - Memory usage
    - Network usage

32) What is the difference between functional and non-functional testing?

Functional Testing	Non Functional Testing
Functional testing is a testing technique which checks that function of the application works under the requirement specification.	Non-functional testing checks all the non-functional aspects such as performance, usability, reliability, etc.
Functional testing is implemented before non-functional testing.	Non-functional testing is performed after functional testing.
It depends on the customer requirements.	It depends on the customer expectations.

Functional requirements can be easily defined.	Non-functional requirements cannot be easily defined.
Functional testing can be performed by manual testing.	Non-functional testing cannot be performed by manual testing.
Following are the types of functional testing: ○ Unit testing ○ Acceptance testing ○ Integration testing ○ System testing	Following are the types of non-functional testing: ○ Performance testing ○ Load testing ○ Stress testing ○ Volume testing ○ Security testing ○ Installation testing ○ Recovery testing

33) What is the difference between static and dynamic testing?

Static Testing	Dynamic Testing
Static testing is a white box testing technique which is done at the initial stage of the software development lifecycle.	Dynamic testing is a testing process which is done at the later stage of the software development lifecycle.
It is implemented at the verification stage.	It is implemented at the validation stage.
Static testing is performed before the code deployment.	Dynamic testing is performed after the code deployment.
Execution of code is not done during this type of testing.	Execution of code is necessary for the dynamic testing.
In the case of static testing, the checklist is made for the testing process.	In the case of dynamic testing, test cases are executed.

34) What is the difference between negative and positive testing?

Positive Testing	Negative Testing
Positive testing means testing the application by providing valid data.	Negative testing means testing the application by providing the invalid data.
In case of positive testing, tester always checks the application for a valid set of values.	In the case of negative testing, tester always checks the application for the invalid set of values.
Positive testing is done by considering the positive point of view for example: checking the first name field by providing the value such as "Akshay".	Negative testing is done by considering the negative point of view for example: checking the first name field by providing the value such as "Akshay123".
It verifies the known set of test conditions.	It verifies the unknown set of conditions.
The positive testing checks the behavior of the system by providing the valid set of data.	The negative testing tests the behavior of the system by providing the invalid set of data.
The main purpose of the positive testing is to prove that the project works well according to the customer requirements.	The main purpose of the negative testing is to break the project by providing the invalid set of data.
The positive testing tries to prove that the project meets all the customer requirements.	The negative testing tries to prove that the project does not meet all the customer requirements.

35) What are the different models available in SDLC?

There are various models available in software testing, which are the following:

- Waterfall model
- Spiral Model
- Prototype model
- Verification and validation model
- Hybrid model

- Agile model
- Rational unified process model[RUP]
- Rapid Application development [RAD]

36) List out the difference between smoke testing and sanity testing and dry run testing?

Smoke Testing	Sanity Testing	Dry Run Testing
It is shallow, wide and scripted testing.	It is narrow and deep and unscripted testing	A dry run testing is a process where the effects of a possible failure are internally mitigated.
When the builds come, we will write the automation script and execute the scripts. So it will perform automatically.	It will perform manually.	For Example, An aerospace company may conduct a Dry run of a takeoff using a new aircraft and a runway before the first test flight.
It will take all the essential features and perform high-level testing.	It will take some significant features and perform in-depth testing.	

37) How do we test a web application? What are the types of tests we perform on the web application?

To test any web application such as **Yahoo, Gmail**, and so on, we will perform the following testing:

- Functional testing
- Integration testing
- System testing
- Performance testing
- Compatibility testing (test the application on the various operating systems, multiple browsers, and different version)
- Usability testing (check whether it is user friendly)

- Ad-hoc testing
- Accessibility testing
- Smoke testing
- Regression testing
- Security testing
- Globalization testing (only if it is developed in different languages)

38) Why do we need to perform compatibility testing?

We might have developed the software in one platform, and the chances are there that users might use it in the different platforms. Hence, it could be possible that they may encounter some bugs and stop using the application, and the business might get affected. Therefore, we will perform one round of Compatibility testing.

39) How many test cases can we write in a day?

We can tell anywhere between 2-5 test cases.

- First test case → 1st day, 2nd day.
- Second test case → 3rd day, 4th day.
- Forth test case → 5th day.
- 9-10 test cases → 19th day.

Primarily, we use to write 2-5 test cases, but in future stages we write around 6-7 because, at that time, we have the better product knowledge, we start re-using the test cases, and the experience on the product.

40) How many test cases can we review per day?

It would be around 7 test cases we write so that we can review 7*3=21 test cases. And we can say that there are 25-30 test cases per day.

41) How many test cases can we run in a day?

We can run around 30-55 test cases per day.

Note: For these types of questions (39-41), always remember the ratio: x test cases we can write, 3x test cases we can review, and 5x test cases we can execute per day.

42) Does the customer get a 100% bug-free product?

1. The testing team is not good
2. Developers are super
3. Product is old
4. All of the above

The correct answer is that the testing **team is not good** because sometimes the fundamentals of software testing define that no product has zero bugs.

43) How to track the bug manually and with the help of automation?

We can track the bug manually as:

- Identify the bug.
- Make sure that it is not duplicate (that is, check it in the bug repository).
- Prepare a bug report.
- Store it in the bug repository.
- Send it to the development team.
- Manage the bug life cycle (i.e., keep modifying the status).

Tracking the bug with the help of **automation** i.e., bug tracking tool:

We have various bug tracking tools available in the market, such as:

- Jira
- Bugzilla
- Mantis
- Telelogic
- Rational ClearQuest
- Bug_track
- Quality center (it is a test management tool, a part of it is used to track the bugs)

Note: Here, we have two categories of tools:

A product based: In the product based companies, they will use only one bug tracking tool.

Service-based: In service-based companies, they have many projects of different customers, and every project will have different bug tracking tools.

44) Why does an application have bugs?

The software can have a bug for the following reasons:

- Software complexity
- Programming errors
- If no communications are happening between the customer and the company, i.e., an application should or should not perform according to the software's needs.
- Modification in requirements
- Time pressure.

45) When do we perform testing?

We will perform testing whenever we need to check if all requirements are executed correctly or not, and to make sure that we are delivering the right quality product.

46) When do we stop the testing?

We can stop testing whenever we have the following:

- Once the functionality of the application is stable.
- When the time is less, then we test the necessary features, and we stop it.
- The client's budget.
- When the essential feature itself is not working correctly.

47) For which and all types of testing do we write test cases?

We can write test cases for the following types of testing:

Different types of testingTest cases

Smoke testing In this, we will write only standard features; thus, we can pull out some test cases that have all the necessary functions. Therefore, we do not have to write a test case for smoke testing.

Functional/unit testing Yes, we write the test case for unit testing.**Integration testing**Yes, we write the test case for integration testing.

System testing Yes, we write the test case for system testing.

Acceptance testing Yes, but here the customer may write the test case.

Compatibility testing In this, we don't have to write the test case because the same test cases as above are used for testing on different platforms.

Ad Hoc testing We don't write the test case for the Adhoc testing because there are some random scenarios or the ideas, which we used at the time of Adhoc time. Though, if we identify the critical bug, then we convert that scenario into a test case.

Performance testing We might not write the test cases because we will perform this testing with the help of performance tools.

Usability testing In this, we use the regular checklist; therefore, we don't write the test case because here we are only testing the look and feel of the application.

Accessibility testing In accessibility testing, we also use the checklist.

Reliability testing Here, we don't write the manual test cases as we are using the automation tool to perform reliability testing.

Regression testing Yes, we write the test cases for functional, integration, and system testing.

Recovery testing Yes, we write the test cases for recovery testing, and also check how the product recovers from the crash.

Security testing Yes, we write the test case for security testing.

Globalization testing

Localization testing
Internationalization testing Yes, we write the test case for L10N testing.
Yes, we write the test case for I18N testing.

48) What is the difference between the traceability matrix and the test case review process?

Traceability matrix Test case review In this, we will make sure that each requirement has got at least one test case. In this, we will check whether all the scenarios are covered for the particular requirements.

49) What is the difference between use case and test case?

Following are the significant differences between the use case and the test case:

Test case Use Case It is a document describing the input, action, and expected response to control whether the application is working fine based on the customer requirements. It is a detailed description of Customer Requirements. It is derived from test scenarios, Use cases, and the SRS. It is derived from BRS/SRS. While developing test cases, we can also identify loopholes in the specifications. A business analyst or QA Lead prepares it.

50) How to test a pen?

We can perform both manual and automation testing. First, we will see how we perform manual testing:

Different types of testing Scenario are

Smoke testing: Checks that basic functionality is written or not.

Functional/unit testing: Check that the Refill, pen body, pen cap, and pen size as per the requirement.

Integration testing: Combine pen and cap and integrate other different sizes and see whether they work fine.

Compatibility testing: Various surfaces, multiple environments, weather conditions, and keep it in the oven and then write, keep it in the freezer and write, try and write on water.

Ad Hoc **testing:** Throw the pen down and start writing, keep it vertically up and write, write on the wall.

Performance testing: Test the writing speed of the pen.

Usability testing: Check whether the pen is user friendly or not, whether we can write it for more extended periods smoothly.

Handicapped people use them.

Reliability testing: Drop it down and write, and continuously write and see whether it leaks or not
Recovery testing Throw it down and write.

Localization testing: Price should be standard, expiry date format.

Internationalize testing: Check whether the print on the pen is as per the country language.

Now, we will see how we perform automation testing on a pen:

For this take a roller, now put some sheets of paper on the roller, then connect the pen to the motor and switch on the motor. The pen starts writing on the paper. Once the pen has stopped writing, now observe the number of lines that it has written on each page, length of each track, and multiplying all this, so we can get for how many kilometers the pen can write.

Conclusion: The End of Manual Testing?

Is Manual Testing Coming to an End? This question is in every mind of the manual tester by seeing the growth of automation testing and we all know automation testing is a step ahead of manual testing in many terms such as automation testing is time efficient etc.

As technology advances, many manual testers are wondering about the future of their job. While automated testing is becoming more popular, manual testing still has a place in the industry. However, manual testing will likely become a "junior partner" and only handle tasks that automated testing cannot yet handle. As technology continues to improve, automated testing is expected to become even more prevalent and eventually replace most manual testing.

THE

END

AUTHOR

NAVIN M S

www.ingramcontent.com/pod-product-compliance
Lightning Source LLC
Chambersburg PA
CBHW082234220526
45479CB00005B/1232